BUSBYS'

A SHOP
FULL OF MEMORIES

Arthur Busby welcoming customers with a cup of tea
on the first day of Busbys' sales

MICHAEL CALLAGHAN & COLIN NEVILLE

BRADFORD MUSEUMS, GALLERIES & HERITAGE

Lift girls c.1931

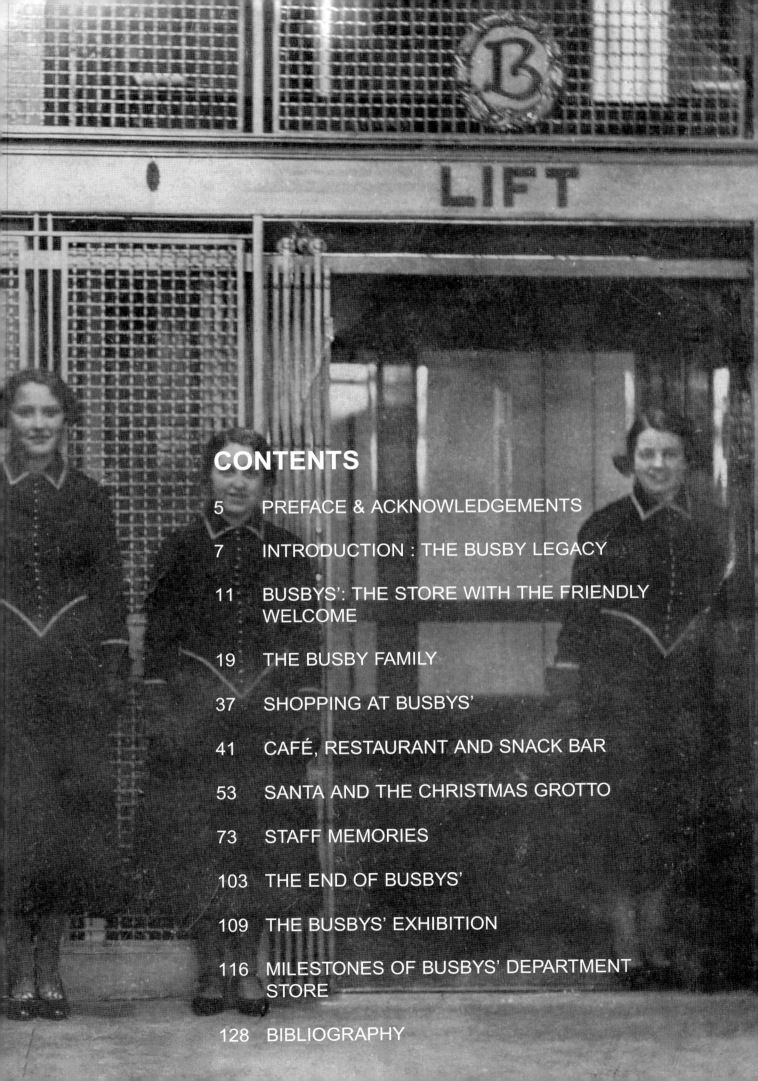

CONTENTS

Published by Bradford Museums, Galleries and Heritage

ISBN 978-0-907734-66-6

Printed by Hart and Clough Ltd , Cleckheaton, Bradford BD19 4TQ
Typeset by Highlight Type Bureau Ltd, Bradford BD8 7HB

Edited by Michael Callaghan and Colin Neville
Project co-ordination by Michael Callaghan
Picture research by David Wood, John Ashton and Michael Callaghan
Editorial assistance by Joan Dearnley

City of Bradford MDC
www.bradford.gov.uk

Preface

Busbys' department store was founded in 1908 and over the next seventy years became one of the most popular stores in Yorkshire. Whilst the building was destroyed by a spectacular fire in 1979, generations of Bradfordians still have special memories of Busbys' – The Store with the Friendly Welcome.

In December 2006 the discovery of photographs showing Busbys' Santa's Grotto back in 1939 led to a small display at Bradford Industrial Museum. To many people the mention of Busbys' immediately reminded them of Busby Santa Claus and the magical Christmas Grotto.

The interest generated in the small display prompted a much larger exhibition in December 2007, which proved to be one of the most popular ever staged at Bradford Industrial Museum. The museum and café became a venue for former staff and customers to meet, renew old friendships and acquaintances, and reminisce about Busbys'.

The department store, or 'shop', as it was affectionately known, was so much more to many people than just a place to work or a place to shop – it was a part of their lives. Busbys' staff and customers have special memories about a time when shopping and life was very different to today.

Thanks must go to everyone who contributed to this book, with a special mention to those who came forward to share their memories and experiences of working and shopping at Busbys'. The enthusiasm and support of everyone connected with Busbys' made this project a pleasure to complete.

The following people and organisations merit particular thanks for their contribution to the publication of this book:

Colin Neville worked as a volunteer at one weekend event and ended up as the chief interviewer for the project. He transcribed all the memories and wrote the introductory chapter on Busbys' Legacy. Without his time and dedication this book would not have been possible.
Amy Booth, Paul Busby and Pat Laycock for their support, knowledge and guidance with everything relating to the Busby family history
Jean Marshall for her wonderful talks about her time working at Busbys'
Maggie Pedley, Mark Suggitt, and staff of Bradford Museums Galleries and Heritage, for their work and support with the exhibition and the book
John Ashton for his work on the photographs and designs for the whole project
David Wood for his help in sourcing the images of Busbys' from the CH Wood Photographic Archive
Alan Hirst for his invaluable assistance with the production of the book
Hannah Haydock and Sarah Lloyd for their help with the layout of the book
Cameron Glennon for his inspiration with the title

Throughout the exhibition and the compilation of this book an overwhelming sense of fun, happiness and togetherness has shone through. We hope you enjoy sharing these memories of Busbys' – The Store with the Friendly Welcome.

Michael Callaghan – Project Co-ordinator

BUSBY'S

HOUSE
MAGAZINE

AUGUST - 1929

" Be civil, just and kind,
Hard work you must not mind,
Your pride in the air must be hurled,
Have patience unto all,
Never let your courage fall,
Then you're bound to get on in the world."

Price Threepence

Front cover of staff magazine

Introduction:
The Busby Legacy

Santa Busby Claus, Mother Christmas and helpers in the famous grotto

Time is a filter that sifts out the chaff of commonplace events to leave a set of dominant impressions; without exception, the memories of Busbys' shared by visitors to the 2007/8 Exhibitions at the Industrial Museum demonstrate this.

For children, the social buzz of the cafés, the rush of the overhead Lamson cash carriers and, above all the Christmas Grotto, made the store a place of wonders. For adults, the recurring and dominant memories of Busbys' are of a shopping emporium, set within a grand Victorian building, where they had come to expect courtesy, attention to detail and quality merchandise offered at competitive prices.

But, as will be seen from the memories in this book, Busbys' was much more than just a place to shop. Ernest Busby and his family had developed over time a unique social and leisure space for both staff and customers, and one with its own strong local identity. Ernest Busby had his family roots in London, but he made Bradford his home – and he quickly recognised the character of the city.

Ernest suited Bradford; he was a canny mixture of continuity and change. He could be direct and beguiling in equal measure; he was a consummate risk-taker; he understood the garment trade, particularly furs, and had an instinct about what would sell, and for how much. He was a mixture of the grand and the unpretentious: quixotic; unquestionably the 'Governor' in word, deed, and appearance; yet always approachable.

The memories in this book will suggest that the term 'customer service' was not just a slogan to Ernest Busby. To him it was something very tangible and profoundly simple in its application. It was about doing decent, effective things. It was about providing chairs for people to sit on when queuing for the sales and providing tea while they waited. It was about repaying the tenacity and patience of the first-comers by allowing them to reserve in advance the bargains they wanted. It was about greeting customers, often by name, and about showing an interest in their lives. And it was about giving them value for their money.

A parade of the Coldstream Guards marching through Bradford in 1961 served as a reminder of the famous Busby logo (see page 33)

The staff followed the Busby family lead, which was made gospel in the House Magazine. Ernest Busby's values, implicit in the theme of 'to do unto others as you would have them do to you', were embedded in the pages of the magazine in many different narrative ways, and reinforced by similar texts from sons, Arthur, Gerald, and Eric. What was deemed to be the right behaviour – and why – was clearly stated in print and practised in daily contact with individuals. The staff knew what behaviour was expected of them in terms of their attitude to customers and to each other.

As the memories in this book suggest, this was not resented or met with cynicism. The staff recognised that the Busby family were not just corporate names, but real people who made their presence felt daily in the store; who saw and noted all; who knew all; and who knew what they wanted from you – and trusted you to deliver it.

From your first day at Busbys' you were considered to be an integral part of this extended family. If you became ill, or ran into personal trouble, you were supported. If you wanted to develop your career, you were encouraged. You were not paid commission, but received a wage that was above the norm for that time. However, like any close family, if you betrayed that trust, or could not share and apply its values, you cast yourself outside its walls.

When the store lost the Busby name in 1973 its identity drained from it. Busbys' had changed, and what had made it special had gone. But by then Bradford had also changed. A thousand economic cuts to manufacturing slowly bled the city of its prosperity and work opportunities for its citizens. And where once a one-stop department store had suited the cultural homogeneity of the area, now individual shops flourished that served the needs of the diverse communities in the city.

By the close of the 1970s, Busbys' was down, but not quite out. The flames that destroyed it drew crowds to the store again for one individual, spectacular and memorable finale.

King George VI and Queen Elizabeth pass a highly decorated Busbys' store on their entry into Bradford, October 20th 1937

Early Family Portrait of Ernest and Amy Busby, with their son, Arthur

Busbys': The Store with the Friendly Welcome

Ernest William Busby, founder of Busbys' department store, was born in 1870 in London. His father, George Busby, a successful publican, apprenticed Ernest to a linen draper, Matthew Rose, in London. The indenture papers record that George paid the handsome sum of £20 for his son to be apprenticed for four years. Embarking on this apprenticeship, Ernest agreed to faithfully serve his master without salary and in return he was instructed in the 'art' of a linen draper. This involved working a twelve to fourteen hour day, six days a week, and sleeping on the premises.

Following his apprenticeship Ernest gained employment as a haberdashery buyer to a West End draper's emporium, one of the pioneers of the modern day department stores. Although individual shops still flourished, stores with multiple departments began to appear in increasing numbers. These department stores were seen as safe and clean environments, with public conveniences, that tempted ladies to shop alone. Large department stores were appearing in the major cities across the country and Ernest was mixing with the well known suppliers and owners of these businesses.

Whilst in London Ernest met Amy Hibbard, who had also been apprenticed to a draper, and they shared many ideals and ambitions. Ernest moved to Owen Owen Limited of Liverpool and became a successful buyer for furs and haberdashery. Amy soon followed and they married in 1895. They settled in Liverpool and had four children. Amy became a constant and important support for Ernest and the family throughout their married life.

Ernest travelled the continent for new ideas and worked closely with the best British suppliers. In 1904 he became Joint Managing Director of Owen Owen and earned the quite substantial salary of £800 a year, plus a bonus. A combination of energy and enterprise resulted in total earnings of £1500 a year for him, equivalent to approximately £86,025 in 2007.

In 1908 Ernest Busby decided to leave Owen Owen, determined to chance everything and start his own business. His contract with Owen Owen had a clause whereby he could not, for a period of five years, start a business within six miles of the Liverpool Exchange. He had spotted the potential for fur and haberdashery sales in Bradford, a city with a significant number of affluent residents. But Ernest noted that the city was far behind others in the way goods were presented and marketed. He commented, "That the wonderful business in furs done in Bradford was not because of the people who handled it, but in spite of them". He invested all his savings in the purchase of stock and fittings and in the lease for an old established, but failing drapery business in Kirkgate.

On 5th October 1908 Ernest Busby opened the doors of his very own store for the first time. He later commented that the change from being Joint Managing Director of a very large concern to owning his 'rabbit hutch' of a shop gave him the greatest thrill of his business life. On the first day of trading so great were the crowds that one policeman was needed to keep order outside, whilst another regulated the pressure inside. At the end of the opening day takings exceeded all expectations. However, following the first month of sales the takings dropped and, with 27 staff to pay, the early days in Bradford were financially difficult for Ernest.

Gradually though, the store came to be spoken of favourably by the ladies well placed in Bradford Society. As a furrier, or dealer and dresser of furs, Ernest became known in the city as the man who was just as enthusiastic about the smaller items of haberdashery as about the more expensive ones.

Ernest and Amy Busby had three sons, Arthur, Gerald and Eric, and a daughter Rita. From a very early age, prior to the First World War, the boys would spend many hours working with their father at the store in Kirkgate learning the trade. The war interrupted these early years of consolidation. Arthur served overseas with the Yorkshire Dragoons, and later the Royal Flying Corps. Eric joined the navy and travelled the world. Gerald was discharged from Her Majesty's Forces on medical grounds and trained in the Local Defence Volunteers (LDVs). Gerald gained experience in the banking world and spent four years with the Midland Bank Head Office – a perfect grounding for the years to come.

Manningham store, 1930 - 1978

After the war Arthur, Gerald and Eric rejoined their father Ernest in the Kirkgate store, and in 1918 Ernest purchased a store in Ilkley, at 5 Brooke Street, which he saw as "an attractive business in one of the loveliest little towns in England". The shop concentrated on selling clothes, and Ernest Busby later wrote:

> After a few days' preparation the shop was opened to a crowd of eager buyers. So great was the appreciation of the Ilkley people of our coming that the door had to be shut at times to regulate the pressure. The little business continued to flourish, and has consistently done so right on for thirty years.

In 1919 Ernest was able to buy the Kirkgate property for £21,000.

Throughout the 1920s the business in Kirkgate expanded into adjoining properties and an additional building was purchased at the rear. The business was built upon the principle of providing customers with what they wanted at competitive prices. Eventually the range of departments and volume of business exceeded the capacity of this extended establishment. Fortunately, in 1929, a great opportunity presented itself to Ernest and his three sons: they learnt that a portion of a larger building in Manningham Lane was to be put on the market. They moved quickly and made an offer, which was accepted.

In 1930 Busbys' (Bradford) was established. It was a private limited company with family members as shareholders and used the now famous trademark of Sergeant Busby and his three men. Ernest Busby became the Chairman with his three sons as directors. By this time Ernest was 60 years old and ready to pass on responsibility to his three sons. Arthur became the front line customer services manager. Gerald was Managing Director and led the development of the new store. Eric was Busbys' buyer, display and advertising man – his closing sale at Kirkgate was so successful that new stock had to be purchased to meet the demand!

Newly opened Manningham Lane store, early 1930s

Following five months of major building work at the site on Manningham Lane Busbys' closed the Kirkgate store on Easter Saturday 1930. The new store opened for business four days later and Amy Busby performed the official opening on Saturday April 26th, supported by her husband and daughter. To Ernest it was a 'Palace of Merchandise'. To Arthur, Gerald and Eric it was a good sized store with great potential.

In contrast to the family optimism, reservations were being expressed within the wider business community as to the suitability of the new site – it being at the top of a hill and away from the city centre. However, fears that people would not go there proved to be unfounded. Busbys' reputation for quality merchandise at affordable prices was now established, and a convenient tram-stop directly outside the store made Busbys' the first port of call for shoppers arriving in the city from the middle-class Bradford suburbs of Heaton, Frizinghall, Saltaire and beyond. At a later date Ernest Busby reflected that the size of the store in Manningham Lane and the range of merchandise resulted in customers coming to the store, not only from Bradford, but from all over Yorkshire.

Throughout the 1930s the range of goods on sale expanded. The store in Kirkgate had concentrated on ladies' wear, linens, haberdashery and furs. Now, in the spacious new surroundings, shoppers lingered to take coffee, tea or lunch in the café, snack bar and two cafeterias. They began asking for things Busbys' did not sell, so Busbys' reacted to this by enlarging the store and their product range. Between 1931 and 1939 the size of the store was multiplied five times by extending into adjoining buildings and doubling the depth, providing space for many more departments, including hairdressing and beauty salons, and a barber shop. Staff numbers increased from 150 to 800. In 1935 a petrol pump service station was opened behind the store, with a car park to cater for the customers with their own transport. In 1937 a customer and in-house laundry was opened and a Power House built, which generated electricity and hot water for the store.

Busbys' was renowned for its Fur Department, which had a large workroom for manufacturing, remodelling and cleaning the furs. The Clothing Yardage Department served the many people in Bradford who made their own clothes, often using patterns bought in the store. They could also buy hats, gloves, trimmings and ribbons from the Millinery and Haberdashery Departments; a dress-making service was also available.

SILVER JUBILEE CELEBRATIONS.
Busbys' gave a firework display in Peel Park, attended by 50,000. Photograph taken by the light of a flare rocket.

Postcard celebrating Busbys' Silver Jubilee, 1958

During World War Two over 460 employees served in the armed forces or on the home front. Six men from Busbys' lost their lives and a war memorial was erected at the Hallfield Road entrance to the store.

After the Second World War the expansion of Busbys' continued, and nearby buildings were acquired to be used as a warehouse and for workrooms. A modern dry-cleaning plant was installed to run alongside the laundry. An ice cream factory opened to complement the in-house and outside catering and bakery activities, which were expanded when the nearby Fountain Hall was acquired as a rendezvous for social events.

In 1953 Buckley's of Harrogate was purchased from the John Lewis Partnership bringing the total of stores with the Busbys' name to three.

The following year Busbys' marked 50 years of business with a firework display in Peel Park, which attracted 50,000 people. A Jubilee Ball was held, attended by over 1,000 past and present employees.

1958 witnessed a major change. A friendly merger was agreed with Mr. John Bedford, Chairman of Debenhams, and a longstanding associate. The merger with Debenhams was seen as a way of securing Busbys' future in the city. An agreement was made to keep the Busbys' name, retain the staff, and to uphold the service to customers.

The merger allowed for further investment to be made and, following structural alterations and refitting on all floors, the 'New Busbys' was unveiled in 1961. The store was serving around 80,000 customers a week.

Over the next decade Busbys' continued to work with Debenhams, but there were changes behind the scenes. In March 1973 Debenhams announced that all its stores would be re-branded with their name. All references to Busbys' and its trademarks disappeared, which caused dismay and protest in the city. Trade continued, but in 1978 Debenhams announced it was closing the Bradford store. Later that year a proposal was made by a supermarket chain to demolish the Victorian facade and replace it with a modern building. This again was met with a public outcry and it was agreed that the grand old exterior would stay. However, on the 30th August 1979, a fire broke out which rapidly spread and gutted the entire building.

Steam engines delivering boilers to the Power House and Laundry
built behind the Manningham Lane store in 1937

17

Ernest W. Busby – founder of Busbys'

The Busby Family

Founder and three sons: (from L-R) Arthur, Gerald, Ernest and Eric

Ernest Busby was a shrewd, tough-minded businessman but he was also driven by a strong set of Christian beliefs. He was a committed Christian and leading member of the Catholic Apostolic Church, and also, in the latter part of his life, a regular worshipper at the parish church of St. Barnabas, Heaton.

In 1934 tragedy struck the family when Amy Busby died of typhoid fever. Eric Busby wrote of the loss of his mother:

> I was devastated beyond anything I had so far suffered in my life to have lost my unfailing champion in such unexpected circumstances. The staff, too, were as shattered as if they had lost a member of the family, and I think it was from that point onward that they began to think of 'Mr. Busby' as their Governor.

In 1944 Ernest Busby married again, to Dorothy Paling, and in time another son, Peter, was born.

In 1957 Ernest William Busby died suddenly, aged 87, at his home, as he prepared to leave home to attend an evening service. Many tributes were paid to the founder of Busbys'. He is buried in Nab Wood Cemetery, Shipley.

Ernest Busby's lifelong values had placed emphasis on doing the fair and decent thing with and to one's neighbours – and expecting the same from them. Ernest's beliefs and values were adopted and applied by his sons and by other members of the family. The three sons complemented each other well: Arthur, the courteous, urbane, public relations man; Gerald, the patrician and financial pillar of the store; and Eric, genial, lively, and with an instinct for finding the right goods for Busbys' customers at the best prices.

The concept of customer service – of putting the interests of the customer first – was the force that drove them all, and which they made clear to staff through their leadership and example and through their writings in the Busbys' House Magazine.

Ernest Busby's first store on Kirkgate between 1908 and 1930

Ernest Busby: (from Busbys' House Magazine)

It is easy enough to be pleasant and nice to customers who are themselves kindly disposed, but customers are not always reasonable beings. Sometimes they feel just cause for complaint, and at other times they feel angry with us without any cause, but invariably they come to give us the full benefit of their wrath. Our natural inclination is to meet wrath with wrath, and to a large extent customers, being human beings, expect it. That is why they are well-equipped with strong indignation, so as to win the first round, as it were. It is our duty and privilege to remember that 'a soft answer turneth away wrath.' We must strive to overcome evil with good and bear in mind the wise saying 'of thy tongue to be the master will thee save from much disaster.' **December 1931**

****

Money is not wealth; wealth lies in giving opportunities to worthy people to make their lives worth living, opportunities of service and of doing something worth while. Busbys' is a prosperous firm because there is in it a spirit of progress and a constant desire to do one's best. There is reason to believe that Bradford is coming back into its own, and there are big things in store for Bradford, so also, we believe there are big things in store for Busbys'. **May 1932**

****

Form the habit of finding fault with your *own* work, rather with that of other people. Look for the best in everybody, honour what is good and strong, imitate what is worth while and, with the breath of kindness, blow the rest away. **July 1934**

GOODWILL

GOODWILL originates in the desire to be of service, and the extent of the goodwill attached to a business depends entirely upon the success or failure in being of service to the community.

Goodwill is therefore purely and simply a term to imply what others think of you, and can be built up in two directions:

1. By the attention shown to customers.
2. By the honourable treatment of wholesale suppliers and manufacturers.

The goodwill of customers is gained by:

- Courtesy
- Sincere interest
- Faithful execution of promises
- Just treatment of complaints
- Truth in advertising and all statements, verbal or written
- Trouble taken to execute special orders

The goodwill of suppliers is gained by:

- Business-like correspondence
- Regular payments
- No returns without adequate reason
- Privileges, if any, requested in a straightforward manner
- No misrepresentation whatsoever

From **Busbys' House Magazine, October 1929**

Arthur Busby c.1930

Arthur Busby: (from Busbys' House Magazine)

The Future of Busbys' Depends on Service

It is confidently expected by the leading men of the trade that in ten years time there will be only two types of drapery establishments – on the one hand, we shall have the super store and syndicate shop; on the other, we shall have the personal, homely type of individual establishment.

It is therefore wise to appreciate the widely differing policies of these two types of businesses and to consider how this tendency affects Busbys'.

The super store or syndicate shop will become more and more efficient, dependent for success upon lavish publicity, alluring display, scientific salesmanship and perfect organisation. Every transaction is automatic, both customer and assistant being merely wheels of a gigantic machine.
This trend of modern business is typical of the hurried, mechanical age but it fails hopelessly to satisfy one very important need of human nature – the need for recognition, personal interest and individual treatment. It is therefore inevitable that side by side with the gigantic organisations there will be homely, personal businesses supported by a loyal clientele, seeking and appreciating personal interest and kindly attention.

Service, therefore, is the only element which will ensure the continuous prosperity of the smaller type of establishment. In years gone by when there was more trade than competition a business could be off-hand and still continue to exist. Today that is quite impossible, as we can well see for ourselves if we look around. It is our duty to continue the policy upon which the Governor [Mr. Ernest Busby] has founded the business and to strive daily and hourly to come nearer perfection.

****

Every business has some kind of personality; good, bad or indifferent. Every department has characteristics which create the particular 'atmosphere' of the department and make it 'individual'. Every display window has characteristics of its own and possesses personality, character, atmosphere – call it what you will, but the effect is the same… [it] possesses the power to create some impression and to achieve some purpose. **July 1934**

****

To promote fellowship in business, always be alive to render service to your colleagues and customers, and let it be of the best and ungrudgingly given. Try to make customers really glad they have come, and want to come again, by being bright and smiling and having a cheery word for all. Never allow a customer to feel any sense of dissatisfaction, and never argue. **November 1934**

Paul Busby: (Son of Arthur Busby)

My grandfather, Ernest Busby, had immense charisma and charm. I was born in 1932 and by then he was already 62; the family called him 'the Pater', and he was very much the pinnacle for holding the family together in World War Two. I was told that in his early days at the Kirkgate store he was something of a go-getter and a tyrant, but I saw a mature, settled, different, loving grandfather. As he went around the store at Manningham it was very much a peregrination, which he did once or twice a day; he was held in very high regard – and people loved him.

He was a Victorian – born in 1870 – brought up with Victorian ethics and Victorian outlook, and those Victorian principles that governed the lives of Empire builders. Yet he fully understood change; he lived through a period of tremendous social change, including two World Wars.

He lived to be 87, and was married, for a second time, to Dorothy, from Sedgefield. She was a lovely lady; she was a great influence on him too, and kept him young. I remember he used some lovely old Victorian expressions like, 'You have to chew your food twenty-two times!' He was a Deacon in the Catholic Apostolic Church at Lansdowne Place, a stone's throw from Claremont, where the family lived when they first came to Bradford.

There was a connection with his religious beliefs and the store. For example, there was a voluntary daily service in the Boardroom, which was more Church of England, as we weren't proselytizing our own beliefs. There was a piano and you often got 40 people there; you couldn't have taken any more. My father and his brothers all had a strong Christian faith right through their lives, and I followed suit.

Grandfather was lovely with the children, and we missed him terribly when he died; and he died very suddenly as he was putting his coat on to go to church. There were 660 people at the funeral at St Barnabas in Heaton

During the War, with Mr. Eric and my father, Mr. Arthur, both being away, the whole of the burden fell on Gerald's shoulders. I was only just a boy then, but it was obvious that Gerald was carrying an enormous burden: what with rationing, and coupons, and blackout, and no petrol. Yet, despite all that, we must have been very good at offering value for money because the store continued to grow right through those difficult years; and it grew at some pace.

My father served in the First World War, which must have been quite horrendous. He was injured when a trench he was in took a shell and seven died; only two survived, including him. But he was peppered with tiny bits shrapnel down his right side. Well after the war, around 1938, I watched my dad shaving one morning and suddenly this shrapnel came to the surface and he put it to one side. I asked him what it was and he said, 'it was a present from the Kaiser!' Incredibly, after World War Two, when he and my mum had another child, my sister, born in 1946, the same thing happened to her when she was a little girl. So he was still shredding shrapnel five decades later.

My father, despite all those awful experiences, was an absolute gentleman. I never heard him swear; I never heard him say anything awful about anybody else; he had a natural charm. He didn't want to be the boss man; his brother Gerald urged him to be the boss in 1930 when they formed the private limited company. But my father said, 'I'm not the right person for the job; you're the right person for the job; you have the brains, the financial expertise; you must do it'. It was the right decision. My father was the front-of-house man; he was wonderful with the public and the staff; his role was about communication and public relations, and represented the store on floor; he was 'Mr. Arthur'.

When he took complaints, suddenly the complainer would be eating out of his hand because he had such charm; he was a lovely, lovely man. He was deeply involved in the Church too, and in another life would have made a good Archdeacon!

As a toddler and a child I would be at Busbys' every week, as when my mother went shopping down at the store I would go with her. So everyone knew 'young Master Paul'. I had been a van boy, unofficially, delivering parcels, but in 1946 when I was fourteen it became legal for me to work. I was on the counter, pretty much a 'dogs-body', on Saturdays during school holidays. In 1950, having left school, I went on to the Woollen Piece Goods counter – which was a major part of the store, as so many people made their own clothes then. I did two years National Service in the Army then went to Bourne and Hollingsworth in London as a management trainee. In 1954 I was back at the store and completed a spell in the Fabric Hall, then went up to the Fashion Floor and became Fashion Floor Supervisor.

The store dominated our lives then, and all these decades later it still does. Busbys' means a lot to me. I can switch on my memory bank and I am back in that building, bustling with life, very labour intensive, with staff everywhere; with designated departments and the Lamson cash carriers zinging around; the restaurant packed with people.

It was 'The Store with the Friendly Welcome'. When customers arrived there was a commissionaire to greet them, and inside they would be swept up in the ambience of the place, with the noise –a bit like a covered market – with all its bustle and activity. We had services of every sort that you could possibly imagine: we made our own ice-cream; we had a dry-cleaning department; we had our own laundry; our own bakery; our own photography department; we were providing a complete service. The café was a meeting place where people had their own tables, booked ahead – and if anyone had not got their table they became very cross!

Gerald Busby with daughter, Amy, c.1940

Gerald Busby: (from Busbys' House Magazine)

[On salesmanship]…All we've got to do is to make it apparent to our customers that we are really delighted to welcome them to our establishment…And then take an enthusiastic and intelligent interest in my lady's requirements: no silly questions, no throwing up the sponge, no irritation with cranks. That is all there is to salesmanship. Simply being decent! **October 1929**

****

There is no denying the fact that one of the most important returns the business can bring to us is the loyalty, confidence and goodwill of the staff. We have it in a large measure, but, as in everything else, we aim for perfection and would like to have your confidence and goodwill entirely. There are a few who do not trust us as friends, possibly owing to difficulties with past employers. Try to learn to trust us more fully, and do not hesitate to bring forward your difficulties. **July 1931**

****

It is far more important to teach people how to live than to teach them how to make a living. To labour for money is the necessity of many, to labour for character is the privilege of all. The development of character is the great worthwhile object of life…Every one of us, with effort and determination, can be persons of distinction in one direction or another, and it is for such persons that Busbys' are searching continually. **December 1931.**

Amy (centre), with father Gerald,
giving prizes at Busbys' sports day, c1950.

Amy Booth: (daughter of Gerald Busby)

My father, during the war years was often down at 'the shop', as we called it. He had to be there; his brothers were away, so off he would go early in the morning and would come back quite late at night. He had started off in a bank, which he said was the most wonderful training he could have had. But he always insisted that Busbys' had the best professional advice they could get from lawyers and accountants; if there was a new development it was always properly looked into and decisions made on other people's professional advice.

The brothers complemented each other; they were incredibly different, and, of course, they didn't always hit it off, but they always managed to come together over a decision of the day; they never had major fall-outs. My grandfather was still active around the store until the time he died, and very much respected. But he had the ability to hand over to the boys, and he didn't interfere; he wanted to know, but let them run the business.

We used to go, my mother and I, and later my brother, always on a Saturday – because that was what you did! We had coffee and then shopped, then had lunch with my aunties and cousins, if they were about. Mr. Baier would show us to our table and my father would appear and have a chat with us. I remember that my father walked around the store every single day – and had his office in what they called 'the glasshouse' in the main office – so he could be seen to be working, and people could approach him. That was important to him, and he would know everybody, and everybody would know him. He was quite a smart figure; he always looked smart.

As a child I always saw him as the 'boss'. It was sort of our shop, but never just ours somehow. All the employees were part of a huge family of people, who were all very friendly, and all got on with each other; the longer serving staff treated us as part of a major family; it had that nice atmosphere.

I remember my father saying that the Haberdashery Department was one of the most important in the store; you have to remember people made their own clothes then. And he felt that for the store to run out of thread to sell was one of the most disgraceful things that could happen. People made these little but important purchases; important to them, and important to Busbys' too, as they returned to buy bigger items.

What did my father expect from staff? Good time-keeping; honesty, of course; friendliness; and a pulling together. He was a very religious person, as were all the family. He was very much a Christian and attended church twice on a Sunday; he played the organ, and was very involved in the church.

My Uncle Arthur was very much the 'customer man' and was out in the front and knew the customers, and he was very good with people. My father was completely hopeless with the 'people side' of the business, because he was far too busy doing other things – but he knew they were important. However, he was a very caring person and would always encourage staff, if they had a serious problem, to come and talk about it, either through the staff office, or direct to him. He did encourage people to open up honestly about problems.

My father always brought work home with him; every day was very long and full for him, which eventually did take its toll on his health. He could get worked up, although he never got desperately cross with any particular person, but he could get very cross at circumstances. However, he would always say 'never let one disaster turn into two'.

Busbys' was a huge place to me, but it had always been there; it was part of my life, so at the time I suppose I didn't think about it that much. All the family were very loyal to Busbys'; there was no reason why we couldn't have shopped elsewhere – but we just didn't!

Amy Booth, (née Busby)

It was a place where you could go and get pretty much anything you wanted or needed. It was never posh! It was very much a family store to serve families – and that is what it did, and was the most important thing it stood for in the city. The fact that it was a business and had to make money was obviously important but it was more there to serve. The thing to remember that 'ladies who lunched' then didn't have cars, so you had to go somewhere where you could get to easily on the bus and meet your friends, outside the home – whereas we meet each other more in our homes now.

I worked there in my late teens, as a secretary in the staff office, and I remember enjoying it and finding the other people I worked with very friendly and affable. However, I didn't get in the way of my father, and he didn't get in the way of me! The work in the staff office gave me an opportunity to go around the store to meet people, as well as interviewing new staff, which I enjoyed doing.

For my father, the fire was the end of a life's work, and he would not have chosen to see it end like that. So although he put on a brave face, it must have very much hurt him.

I am certainly proud to be a member of the Busby family and enjoy the fact that there has always been this 'wider family' out there who have always been very loyal to Busbys', and still speak well of Busbys' today.

Eric Busby c.1930

Eric Busby: (from Busbys' House Magazine)

To you [commercial salesmen] who find us flinty and unyielding, do not take it as a personal grievance; wait until you have a line that will soften our hearts.

Let me tell you of a man who called on me, and called, and called, but never got his order book into the light of day. He told me a long time afterwards that he went out of Busbys' saying "I will sell this little d...l something". This is the spirit, and he did! We have had some big deals together since then; the last invoice I passed from his firm was for £380, and confidence had grown to such an extent that the goods were purchased over the telephone without my seeing them. Were they all right? They were! They were all sold. **August 1929.**

****

[To the sales staff] You have been thoughtful and attentive to your customers at Kirkgate. You must be even more so in Manningham Lane; and why? Simply this: whereas in Kirkgate hundreds of customers have come because we are conveniently situated in the centre of Bradford. The premises in Manningham Lane must be made so inviting that customers who have hitherto regarded Busbys' merely as a convenience will choose to climb the hill rather than go elsewhere…Now this opportunity will be the big chance – the few minutes that each customer will give us to make good impressions. The buyers will leave no stone unturned in providing the right value: you will be expected to give the right type of service: co-operation will prove our cause and we shall win the day. **March 1930.**

Eric after receiving his MBE for Services to the Community,
in 1978, with his children, John and Pat

Pat Laycock, (née Busby) c.1930

Pat Laycock: (daughter of Eric Busby).

The staff could always talk to my grandfather Ernest if they had a personal problem. He would give them all his attention – he was a Personnel Officer without really knowing it! By the time I have memories of him he would have been more or less retired from a hectic business life, but my mother would talk about how, when he was younger, he would rush about as if he was enthused by his own enthusiasm. He was a bit of a showman, sometimes keeping his white fur-workroom coat on over his smart business suit in the manner of a surgeon visiting the wards. Customers were impressed! He was never prejudiced about people from other cultures; perhaps that is because of his travels around Europe, he accepted all people for what they were and had tremendous sympathy for refugees.

My father, Eric, had a flair for anything artistic, but being an artist would have been unthinkable to the family in those days, so he did what his father thought best. He had a gift for publicity and blowing the shop's trumpet – to the great embarrassment of his mother who was a rather retiring person and couldn't stand razzmatazz. When he retired from the shop in 1959 he founded a successful art gallery so he made it to the art world in the end.

My father was away for six years during World War Two. All the staff would ask after his welfare and were very kind to my mother, brother and myself. When he came back in 1945 everything was in short supply, but it was a great time for getting surplus government stock, so he could organise fantastic sales! I remember that the departmental buyers had real responsibility and would purchase merchandise according to the needs of the customers. They were almost like members of the family and some of them were enormously respected, for example the toy buyer Mr. Denison and the fur buyer Mrs. Thompson, but Busbys' could not have succeeded without the loyalty of all the staff.

The Busbys' soldiers logo. The logo represents Ernest Busby, founder of the store,
followed by his three sons, Arthur, Gerald and Eric.
The four soldier emblem was first used in 1928, and became inseparable in every facet of the business.
Ernest took much delight in the significance of the four soldiers.
He used to explain that it was a symbol of:
Unity – the soldiers are all in step.
Progress – they are all on the march
Uprightness – they are all straight and erect

Fabric department

Shopping at Busbys'

Busbys' targeted its business at the growing ranks of the lower-middle classes in Bradford, although its Fur Department attracted affluent customers from across and beyond the city. Throughout most of Busbys' tenure in Bradford (1908 – 1973), the city was a relatively affluent place, with textiles and engineering manufacturing still economically buoyant until the late 1960s. As noted earlier, the store became known, not only as a general shopping emporium but as a social meeting place for Bradfordians. They could meet and socialise in the library, cafés, hairdressing and beauty salons, and at the record counter. Parents would bring their children to Busbys' on shopping trips on a Saturday, with the promise of a special treat of lunch in the café. Brides could buy their wedding dresses at Busbys', and later have a wedding meal prepared, served, and their futures toasted, in nearby Fountain Hall, opened by the store in 1954 as a social venue.

****

May I thank your assistant who served my wife and me last Saturday afternoon. Her kindness to us was simply magnificent. She was attentive, kind, thoughtful and goodness in herself – a credit to your firm. It is the first time we have had the pleasure of entering your place and we were delighted. No wonder you have to increase your establishment if all your assistants are like her. From **Busbys' House Magazine, May 1934**

The things I remember: our laundry being collected by the Busbys' van from home on a Monday and delivered back on a Thursday; taking a broken watch into the store and they sent it all the way to Scotland to be repaired; Children's wear at sale time was a big attraction. Busbys' was renowned to have 'something for everyone' **Anonymous: 'regular customer', aged 82**

The Busbys' store was known as the 'Harrods of the North'. You could buy anything in that store – furniture, clothing, toys – even fur coats. Mr. Busby wanted shopping to be an enjoyable experience, and even in the 1940s it had a dedicated crèche to help mothers have a little time to themselves when shopping. Very few stores today could match the shopping experience of the Busby store. **Janet Wild**

I bought a dining table and chairs from the Furniture Department, which lasted from 1956 to 2006. A wardrobe mirror I bought, which was chipped on the back, was replaced by the Manager, who brought a replacement wrapped in a blanket in his own car. Service! **Anonymous.**

Almost 50 years ago I bought my first transistor radio from Busbys'. I remember paying for it with a large bag of threepenny bits. My mother and I had to leave the bag with the cashier as she needed time to count them all! **Jill Riley** (née Roberts)

I got married in 1956 and we rented a flat on Manningham Lane. The landlady lived on the ground floor and nowadays you would recognise in her the first symptoms of dementia. One day she went to Busbys', shopping. The store rang up and said there was an elderly lady shopping on the underwear counter. I said 'is that a problem?' The answer was 'no madam, but the lady insists on trying the garments on at the counter'. I said, 'well, why was that a problem?' The manager said, 'well madam, it is the knickers counter – and she has three pairs on!' So I had to hotfoot down to fetch her back and pay for three pairs of knickers. **Shirley Aldous** (née Hague)

I bought my first pair of tights at Busbys' one day after school in the 1960s. Another memory is buying a trendy mini-dress there. I thought it was fab. We also held our wedding reception at Fountain Hall in 1969 and I can still remember the lovely food we ate. **Margaret Herd** (née Frampton)

Staff waiting to serve behind Hosiery counter

The millinery department at sales time

My mother bought my wedding veil for me in 1967. I remember sitting at a kidney shaped dressing table to try it on and feeling very special. **Pauline Chapman**

My happiest memory of Busbys' is buying my wedding dress in 1968. They had just finished putting it into a display but were happy to take it out for me. The staff were lovely. I watched it burn down from the back garden of our house. I wish it was back now; there's nothing else remotely like it. **Susan Ellerton**

I remember being taken to Busbys' as a child and the excitement of the trip with the cash containers whizzing round our heads. **Pam Lofthouse** (née Robertshaw)

Birthday treats and special occasions were often celebrated by a trip to Busbys'. After a good look round, the highlight was tea in the café, where Mr. Busby always came to each table to talk to the children. I always loved the window displays and in later years became a window dresser myself. It makes me realise what a forward-thinking business this was. Disney World may seem like a new concept – but Busbys' did it all before.
Doreen Baxter

Busbys' was the start of our day-out in town. We got off the bus from Saltaire and used to go straight into the shop – with the wonderful smell of perfumes and the friendly staff. **Rosemaree Rawnsley** (née Hughes)

I well remember visiting Busbys' every Saturday when I was young. Mum used to have her hair done at the hairdressing salon there whilst Dad wandered around the library. Afterwards we'd have something to eat, admiring the mannequins as they wandered past in the latest fashions. **Manjit Singh Pattar**

Customers from Skipton, c1931

I must have spent every Saturday in my early teens browsing round Busbys'. I probably spent half my pocket money, which was two shillings, there; goodness knows what I bought. I probably still have some of my purchases. I was fascinated by the tube system of payment. At least you could guarantee you got the right change and a receipt. I would spend hours looking in the windows even when the store was closed. My wish was to become a window dresser. **Christine Anne Watkin** (née Carr)

My favourite memory of Busbys' is of my sister, Wendy Clegg, who worked in the perfumery department as 'Miss Revlon'. She always wore a turquoise dress – the Revlon uniform. She had many regular customers, two of whom proposed to her! Sadly Wendy died in 2001. **Sandra McCullough**

Being Art students we walked to Busbys' and bought buttons to make our own earrings. We also bought remnants from the material department, which as dress designers we made up for the college fashion show. **Biddy Litten**

I remember as a little girl going to Busbys' with my Gran. She used to buy me ribbons for my hair from Haberdashery on the ground floor. It was like Pandora's box for a little girl and I loved looking at all the lovely buttons. **Karen Taylor**

I met Johnny Dankworth in Busbys' record shop. He was promoting his hit record 'Three Blind Mice'. I also remember an escapologist – Shahid Malik – being chained up and immersed in a huge tank of water on the top floor. Happy memories. **Derrick K. Smith**

Café, Restaurant and Snack Bar

I well remember the head waiter at the café was an Austrian whose name was pronounced Byer, but spelt Bieur or Baier. We had many chats together. He arrived in Bradford to work at the Midland Hotel and his intention was to learn English and then travel before returning home. But he served so many businessmen, who had connections with Germany, and got on so well with everyone, that he stayed. Ruefully he mentioned the time he arrived in Bradford from Austria. He got off the train at Forster Square Station and asked a taxi-man to take him to the Midland hotel. They travelled for quite a while. The next morning he was dumbfounded to find that the station was next to the hotel and he really had been 'taken for a ride!' **Winifred Firth**

Head Waiter Charles Baier

One of our most successful ventures was the café... we also introduced a snack bar for quick meals where the cooking was done behind the circular counter by classy, glamorous girls. Not long after its opening the café came to be presided over by an exceptional head waiter called Charles Baier who had been in the employ of the Grand Duke Franz Joseph. By the time I met him he was a refugee working in a commercial hotel in Kirkgate, where his charming Austrian manners were wasted.

How pleased he was when I offered him a job, particularly as we increased his wages many times over from the 16/- a week he had been earning. As well as ensuring that seating and service were excellent, he brought high chairs for children, or cushions for grown-up children, and enquired after the welfare of everyone with such interest they all felt they were Busbys' most important customers.
Eric Busby: (from 'Letters from Eric Busby to his Grandchildren')

Having thoroughly enjoyed an excellent lunch, as usual, imagine my horror on finding that my loose cash amounted to a few coppers and that I had left my notecase at home! Not a nice situation under any circumstances, but imagine my feelings considering I am a stranger and entirely unknown to your staff. Extraordinary pictures flashed through my mind of myself being thrust forth by an indignant manager or even leaving the building in charge of a policeman!

However, taking my courage in both hands, I approached your Mr. Baier and imagine my astonishment when after my first whispered words of explanation and apology, he smilingly and without the slightest hesitation took my bill and assured me all would be well. That was all – no lengthy explanations, no questions, why, he didn't even ask my name and address.

I assure you, Gentlemen, I am extremely grateful for this splendid example of friendliness and tact which confirms the opinion I already had of your firm and your staff.

From: **Busbys' House Magazine, July 1934**

Edna Broadbent (3rd from right) with waitresses from Busbys',
15th September, 1933

I was born in a mining village in South Yorkshire, but there wasn't any work for girls then so my Dad took me down to London and I went to stay with my grandma. I found a job as a waitress at the Lyons Corner House, Piccadilly. After a year working there I was a due for a holiday so I came back to Yorkshire, but didn't want to go back, so I found a job in a private hotel in Bradford. But someone told me they got more wages at Busbys' if you worked as a waitress. I went there and they set me on straight away. This was 1932. I settled in very well and I liked it alright.

There was some nice staff and they were friendly to me; they made me feel at home. I met my husband, Tom Broadbent, who worked there. He came one time and said 'would you liked to go out to the pictures with me'. But I said 'I'm not going out with you', as I knew he was engaged to another girl, called Edith! He went away a bit crestfallen, but he came back again and says 'will you go out with me now as I've finished with Edith?' So this time I had no excuse and we started going out. We had a tandem; you should have seen me pedalling!

The restaurant was a nice place to work. I looked after 12 customers. You wanted to make people come back to Busbys' to have another meal. Let's say they came from a village on the outskirts of Bradford, and they've come a long way, and done their shopping, and now they want a good meal and they don't want people being off-hand. So you were friendly with your customers. If there was something on the menu and they had had it the time before, you could remember it and say there's so-and-so on the menu to remind them, in case they wanted it again. And they appreciated it. **Edna Broadbent** (née Wilce)

Kitchen staff preparing meals, and waitresses ready to serve

In the café the waitresses had the same station all the time and on Saturday it was completely booked with families coming to the same waitress. During the week the businessmen would come and if the waitresses knew there was something on the menu and that 'their gentlemen' particularly liked it, they would go in the kitchen and say 'will you be sure to save some for one of my gentlemen; he's coming in at 1 o'clock today'. **Jean Marshall**

In the 1940s, as a special treat, we came to Busbys' for afternoon tea – scones and jam. Mother seemed to know Mr. Ernest and when he was there (checking all was well) he used to come and ask me if I had been a good girl. I, of course, always said 'yes', and he gave me a threepenny bit, of which I have kept three. I loved his wing collar and his slicked-back hair; he always was straight and immaculate. I was quite in awe of him.
Shirley Aldous (née Hague)

I remember the restaurant in the late fifties and early sixties. My parents and I had lunch there every Saturday. You could get a three-course meal for three people, with coffee, and still have change from a 10/- note (or in today's money, a 50p coin!). We sat at the same table every week and our waitress was Miss Florence Johnson, whom we got to know quite well and who knew us and what food we liked. If you ordered the hors d'oeuvres, you could watch it being made up by the expert lady at the snack bar: it was almost a complete meal in itself.

On some days mannequins used to parade around the restaurant displaying elegant fashionable dresses and coats. At some lunchtimes 'Mr. Gerald' Busby would be in attendance, greeting customers and making sure they were well looked after. He knew many by name, including my father. 'Mr. Gerald' was a man of enormous presence and commanded much respect from customers and staff alike; it was an honour to meet him. While my parents had coffee, I would be allowed to visit the basement toy department by myself. This was a real treat because there was always something new to see. You could hire cine films to play at your family's children's parties. We hired a cartoon film called 'Happy Scouts' and we liked it so much I had it at my party at least three years in succession! I'd love to see it again. **Judy Blezzard**

Behind the scenes – staff enjoying a slice of cake

My favourite memory of Busbys' was the beautiful restaurant at the top of the store. I was about five years old and my Auntie Gladys and family took me there for Christmas dinner. It was very lavish (posh, I thought!). I was also amazed at the ladies powder room. I loved the hand lotions. **J. Morton**

My mum worked in the kitchens for many years, and during the school holidays I was sometimes allowed to go and help in the still room clearing tables, or to help the ladies in the sewing room. The atmosphere was wonderful – everyone working really hard and loving it. I remember that my older sister and mum talked about the Princess Royal visiting Fountain Hall for lunch and they served her. Busbys' was terrific and had everything – we'll never see its like again. **Janet Rhodes**

I remember as a little boy my old aunt Alice taking me and one of my sisters to the snack bar and saying she was going to treat us to Welsh Rabbit. I was horrified at the thought of eating rabbit –I didn't know it was cheese on toast! **John Walter**

My earliest memories of Busbys' were those of being treated, alternatively with my sister Renee, to have tea in the café on Friday afternoons during school holidays. I always chose sausage and chips with, treat of treat, tomato sauce. **Anonymous**

As a young boy my mother used to regularly take me to Busbys' cafeteria for my dinner. I remember it well: lots of stainless steel and curtained partitions for wedding parties etc. I particularly liked the roast potatoes, swimming in sticky beef dripping, with lots of meat stuck to them. **Geoff Crossley**

Front cover of a Christmas Menu

Choyce of ye Soupe
(Warme tis for one and alle)

Turkeys servyd with
ye Savourie Balles and
Sausage Tomatoe

Choyce of ye Vegetabells

Christmasse Pudynges of England
or
Ye Tarte of Mincemeate

Sauce flavoured with Rum from
Jamaica

Ye Cheese and Biscuits
or
Coffee

2/-

# of Fare

Choyce of ye Soupe
(Goode for alle men and maydens)

Fushe - - Fryed Sole
with ye Sauce of Parslie

Pork from ye Northe Countree
Savourie of lyke mannere and Apple Sauce

Choyce of ye Vegetabells

Christmasse Pudynges of England
or
Ye Tarte of Mincemeate
Sauce flavoured with Rum from
Jamaica

Ye Cheese and Biscuits
or
Coffee

2/6

BUSBYS'

CHILDREN'S

MENU

LUNCH MENU

Choice of Soup
Yorkshire Pudding and Gravy
One Vegetable or Potatoes
Milk Pudding or
Stewed Prunes and Custard

11d.

Roast Breast of Chicken and
Vegetables

1/3

Roast Beef and Vegetables

9d.

Steamed or Fried Plaice and
Vegetables

1/-

TEA MENU

Tea or
Hot or Cold Milk

Buttered Teacake

Fresh Fruit Salad
and Jelly

Jam Sponge Cake

6d.

Tea or Horlick's Malted Milk
Chips
Fried Fillet of Whiting and
Parsley Sauce
White or Brown Bread and Butter
Iced Bun

or

Tea or Chocolate Horlick's
Children's Fish Cake and Chips
Brown Bread and Butter
Swiss Roll

or

Tea, Milk or Lemonade
Rainbow Sandwiches
Cream Trifle   Fancy Biscuit

8d.

Children's Menu

48

Café c.1960

BUSBYS
DOUBLE DECKER
SANDWICHES

TOMATO EGG and CHICKEN

TOMATO CHEESE and HAM

BEEF, LETTUCE,
CHEESE and TOMATO

Snack Bar, c1937

The Magic of Santa's Grotto

Santa and the Christmas Grotto

Santa in Cinderella's kitchen, 1939

Mention the name Busbys' and Santa's Christmas Grotto immediately springs to mind, and a visit to it became an eagerly awaited annual event for thousands of Bradford families.

However, the first Busbys' Grotto did not feature Father Christmas and was set up in the basement at the store in Kirkgate, where a setting of Little Red Riding Hood's cottage was built. A motor car was hired, upon which was built another cottage, and Little Red Riding Hood sat outside the cottage as the motor car drove around the city and beyond. Bradfordians had never seen anything quite like this before and children with their parents flocked from across the district to see the Grotto and to receive a present.

In time, Father Christmas came to the Busbys' Grotto and his arrival in the city, complete with his retinue, including Mother Christmas, a Christmas Fairy, reindeer, and accompanying brass band, sent thousands on to the streets to cheer him on his way and to gather the sweets thrown to the crowds lining the route:

> The crowd which met Father Christmas in Bradford was so great that it was only with extreme difficulty that he was able to force his way through. Father Christmas attracted one of the largest crowds that Bradford has ever seen – certainly the largest Busbys' have ever known. (Busbys' House Magazine No.18, December 1935)

Planning for the Grotto started in June of each year and was taken seriously by the staff. In the November 1934 issue of Busbys' House Magazine there is an article about the toy season which predicts how busy Father Christmas will be and expresses some concern about how the queues will be dealt with. This was resolved by making the Grotto a place of wonder to the children who queued along its length: subdued lighting, waterfalls, animated models, snowflakes falling, Santa's Fairy, and Little Red Riding Hood's sweet shop, all made the wait to meet Santa more bearable. At the end of the corridor they finally met and spoke with Santa and received a gift from him.

Snow White in Busbys' Grotto.

CHRISTMAS, 1938.

Father Christmas, Mother Christmas, Snow White and Tommy Busby.
A CORNER OF BUSBYS' SNOW WHITE GROTTO, CHRISTMAS, 1938.

Christmas Postcard, 1938

I have wonderful childhood memories of Santa and his Grotto. Queuing for Santa seemed to take hours, but there was so much to look at. It all seemed so magical. I remember getting a toy whistling kettle and a badge saying 'I saw Santa at Busbys'. Nothing these days matches it! **Bev Mathers**

Visiting Father Christmas in Busbys' Grotto was the highlight of my year. The thrill and excitement never faded and really made my childhood Christmas a joy for the next 12 months. After seeing Santa, a drink and waffles in the café was the order of the day. I can still taste the cream and treacle, yum, yum! Fond memories.
Helen A. Widdas (née Crossland)

I remember visiting Santa's Grotto at Busbys' as a child. It was the highlight of my Christmas. We always went on a Saturday morning. The queues to get in were very long, but the wait was worth it. Now I live in Hong Kong and see lots of wonderful Christmas displays, but nothing compares to the magic of Busbys' Christmas Grotto!
Anonymous

There was only one 'real' Santa – and that was at Busbys'. The Grotto: it has to be the best ever. I was so upset when it closed down. I went every year from 1966 onwards – I particularly remember the long queues to get in the door and then what seemed to be the endless corridor of 'magic' before arriving and sitting on Santa's knee. Happy memories indeed. **Laura Campbell**

The Busbys' store was always busy – but Christmas was special. Mr. Busby would ensure that Santa's Grotto was every child's dream. Although Santa was not promising computers and MP3 players – the children were happy with dollies and teddy bears wrapped in colourful paper. **Janet Wild**

Christmas Postcard, 1938

Santa Busby Claus and Mother Christmas setting off through Bradford, to Busbys' Grotto, c1930s

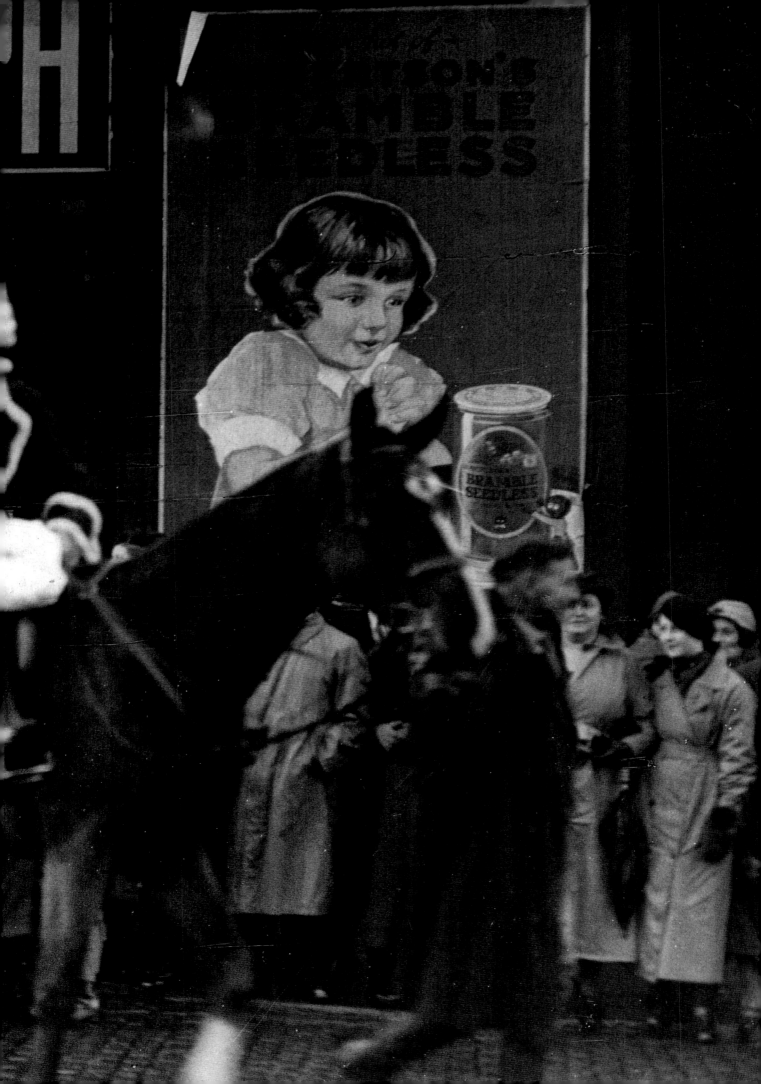

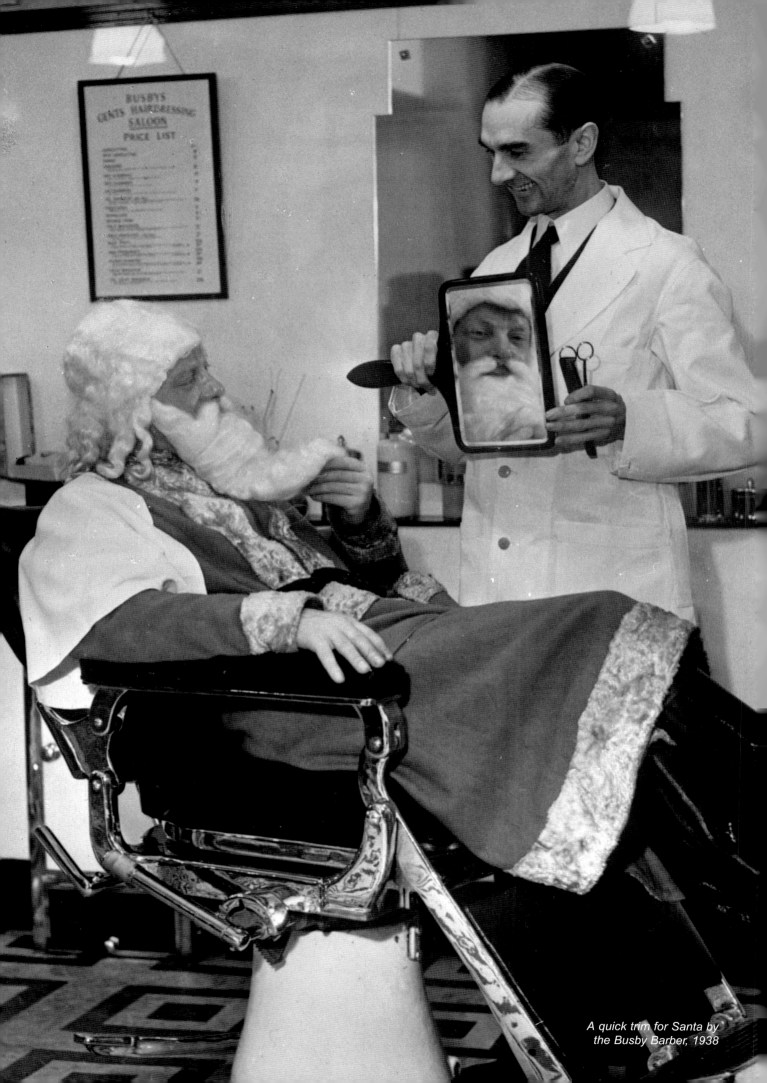

A quick trim for Santa by the Busby Barber, 1938

*An early photograph of Santa Busby Claus ringing his bell
(Eric Busby on the left waving)*

I really believed I'd stepped into Santa's magical kingdom when I visited Busbys' in the early 1950s. I used to be so worried that Mum and Dad wouldn't get me back home in time before Santa set off on the reindeer. I was given a little bear by Santa and named him 'Rupert'. I still have him; very battered, as he is over 50 years old. **Sheila Ognissanti** (née Rhodes)

I have fond memories of the Christmas Grotto, being a child in the 1950s. It was very exciting waiting in the queue to see Santa; the Grotto was the most magical place to go through – with Santa, Mother Christmas, and the fairy sat waiting at the end. In the early 1970s I also brought my children to see Santa. **Marlene Harwood**

My memory is being taken to see Santa Claus when very small. My memory is a huge display of lights and tinsel and magic. We had to walk down paths and over bridges, pull strings, and glitter snowed down on us. It seemed as though we walked for ages before we saw Santa… that walk and the magic has never been equalled in any display since. **A. Wallace**

I will always remember Santa's Grotto. The walk through the Grotto was a magical experience and to find Santa waiting for us to ask what we would like was all we dreamed of. **Angela McHugh**

Christmas time – I brought my three children to visit Santa and they were thrilled – the magic of the long walk to the Grotto; things to pull – with resulting squeals and grunts – then the Man himself. As a special treat we had lunch in the café afterwards and Santa would take a walk and talk to the children. A special place. **Margaret Clark**

Santa Busby Claus and Mother Christmas in
Cinderella's Kitchen at Busbys'   Christmas 1939

Judy Blezzard meeting Santa Busby Claus, c.1950

I went to Busbys' Grotto for the last time when I was 9 years old in 1971. I had to fill in a book with my name and address so Santa knew where to come. I asked for 'Tiny Tears' and he gave me a gold wallet with a gold pen and note-book. I loved it and treasured it. The best Christmas memories were Busbys'. **Judy Hurley**

As a child I loved Santa's Grotto and I remember meeting Sooty and friends when Harry Corbett put on one of his first shows in the 1950s. He surprised the first few rows of his audience with his water-pistol. I had Sooty and Sweep puppets for many years afterwards. **Anonymous**

[The Grotto] It was paradise. As soon as Plot Night was over we'd be counting the days until it was time for Santa Busby Claus and his entourage to drive in splendour along Manningham Lane and enter his domain. I think that children lost their sense of wonder much later in those days. My belief in Santa came to a sad end. Pedlars in 'Santa' costumes used to carry trays of goods and ply for business in Kirkgate. One day we saw two of them fighting over the same pitch. Despite my parents' horrified reassurances that these weren't real Santas (the real one was of course in his grotto at Busbys') my disillusionment was complete. I wept sorrowful tears, much like those that came on hearing that Busbys' was no more. Another of life's certainties had gone. **Judy Blezzard**

I must have been the only child who didn't enjoy the visit to Santa's Grotto. I was aged about 3, and when we finally reached Santa he said, "what do you want little girl?" I replied, "I want to get out of here!" **Anonymous**

The first time I had the opportunity to visit Santa Claus was at Busbys'. My brother, who was 7 years older than me, took me down on a Saturday morning. We queued for what seemed liked hours. We were winding our way along this corridor and there were things to look at and things to do all the way along: little windows, and things that moved. It was so exciting; I would be about 5 years old then. We got closer, and closer, and eventually got to the head of the queue. But I was over-awed by this vision of Santa Claus sitting there. He beckoned me to come near him, but I wouldn't go I was so overwhelmed. He tried to ask me what I wanted for Christmas, but I burst into tears! My brother was furious as we had queued all that time. But when it came to the big moment, I chickened out! But I did get a gift – a little doll's tea-set, which I had for years. **Margaret Lee**

Christmas Postcard, 1939

Santa and Mother Christmas on horseback in Bradford, c1935

From the Home of Father Christmas

TELEPHONE 23456
TELEGRAMS 'SANTA POP'

IN **BUSBYS**

TOYLAND GROTTO

My dear little Friend,

How pleased I was to have your letter, brought straight to my beautiful red and white and gold Grotto at Busbys' by the postman.

We have been oh! so busy in Toyland ever since last Christmas, hammering and sawing and banging to make this year's toys - and Busbys' have been busy making me a smashing Old Tyme Grotto so that I could come and see my little friends again. The ladies look so pretty in their lovely crinolines - just like Grandma used to dress, or let's see, perhaps her Grandma.

The dollies have come all the way from Toyland in a Hansom Cab and the gnomes are busy with their Christmas party - even the Snowman outside is dancing and everybody's having a wonderful time. And there's the old Tyme Shoppe where the gnomes bought the goodies for their party - Mother Christmas thinks she'll do her shopping there too. But just now she's busy writing down all you want for Christmas in my BIG RED BOOK so I won't forget a thing.

Mother Christmas, Fairy Starlight, Queenie my reindeer, and me all send all our love and will see you again Christmas Eve. Mind you keep your eyes tight shut.

Love and kisses

SANTA CLAUS

From the Home of Father Christmas

IN **BUSBY'S**

TELEPHONE 23456
TELEGRAMS 'SANTA POP.'

FAIRY GROTTO

My dear Little Friend,

Mother Christmas and I have been having a chuckle about your extra special letter and now I must copy down all you want just to make sure about everything. I have to be jolly careful about special orders — I'll do the best I can for you, for certain, and you won't be disappointed.

The postman keeps popping in with more and more letters, but I like writing replies - it keeps me out of mischief in the evenings and it's better than looking at T.V.

It is a lovely fairy sort of night here. I have just been for a walk round the waterfalls and made sure that everything is in working order for tomorrow when I expect lots and lots more children to come and see me. It's lovely, I would not miss coming to Busbys for anything. I go to the Cafe every tea-time too. I might see you there sometime.

I know where you live now and I am looking forward to seeing you on Christmas Eve. Be very good and leave the rest to me and my magic.

My favourite reindeer Queenie, and Fairy Starlight want me to send their love to you.

              Lots of love.

              SANTA CLAUS.

My dear little Friends,

I thought I would write you a little note to tell you that here I am again at Busbys, having a fine time and looking forward to Christmas.

I am very happy in my Christmas Circus Grotto this year, with exciting things going on all around me! The clowns have had a thrilling journey from Toyland in their veteran motor car. It broke down quite a few times, you know.

The lions are a little bit noisy with their roaring, but they're great big show offs and not at all fierce, really. The clown on the tightrope frightens me a bit though, in case he should lose his balance and fall – but I'm sure he won't. Just fancy being able to train horses like the Ringmaster can; don't you think he's clever?

Mother Christmas and Fairy Starlight are reminding me to send their love to you, and Queenie, my reindeer, says to be sure and be asleep when we call with your presents on Christmas Eve. Remember to be very, very good, because I can't call on not-so-good boys and girls, but I'm sure you won't be naughty, will you?

Lots of love from

SANTA CLAUS

From the Home of Father Christmas

TELEPHONE 23456
TELEGRAMS 'SANTA POP'

IN BUSBYS
TOYLAND GROTTO

My dear little Friend,

How nice of you to send me such a lovely letter. I have enjoyed reading it.

I have been talking to Fairy Starlight and she and Mother Christmas have helped me with the list of all the things you would like most for Christmas. We don't promise but will do our best and will think of one or two unexpected presents for surprises, as well.

I am looking forward to Christmas just as much as you. I know your house. What a happy and exciting time you will have at waking up time on Christmas morning.

I am writing this letter in my Grotto home at Busbys! It is night time and I've just been playing with my magic Alpine railway, which runs in and out the mountains and across a viaduct. I have a fountain and some pretty birds and goldfish, and clowns to play with too. I am having a good time. Queenie my reindeer has just gone to sleep and I am thinking of all the boys and girls who have been to see me, and those who have written to me, like you. Now it's my bedtime too.

Be ever so good until Christmas.

LOTS OF LOVE

SANTA CLAUS

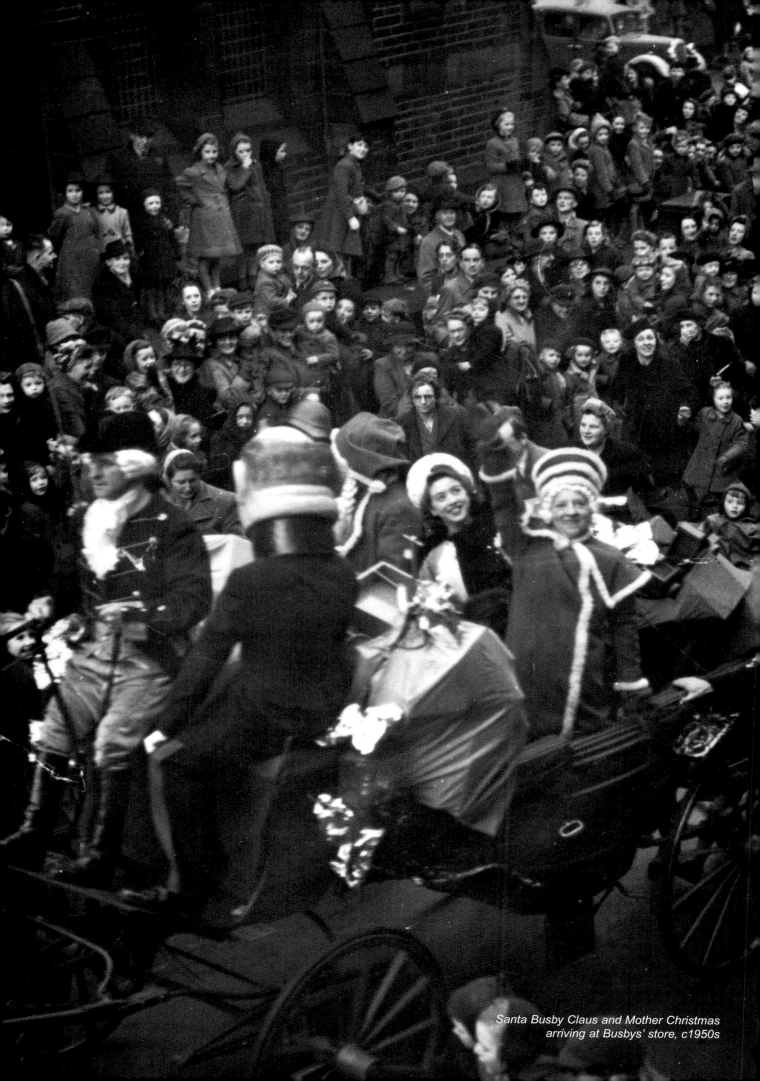

*Santa Busby Claus and Mother Christmas
arriving at Busbys' store, c1950s*

Staff Memories

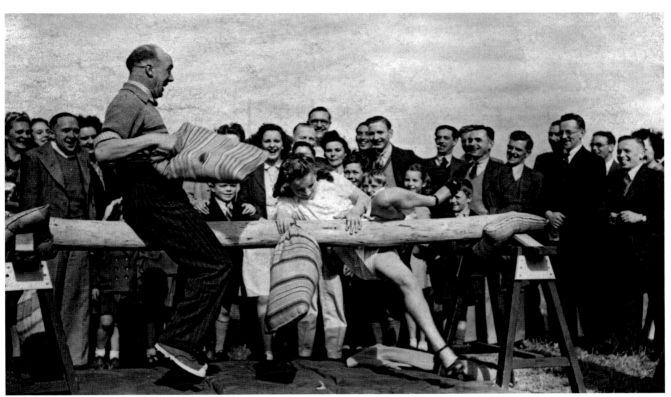

Greasy Pole at Busbys' staff sports day, c1950

At one point, in the early 1950s, over a thousand people were employed at Busbys' and an extensive welfare and social support network developed to encourage a feeling of common purpose and team effort. Sports clubs, amateur dramatics, store dances and annual trips gave the staff a chance to meet and make friends; many Busbys' employees met their marriage partners in this way.

Sack race at Busbys' staff sports day, c1950

Staff at Ernest Busby's 80th birthday party, November 15th, 1950.
Jean Marshall, née Denby (centre standing)

Busbys' was family: it was a family business, with a family feeling; the staff were made to feel part of a big family. The Directors knew the staff, and the staff knew the Directors. You knew they were good men. These days you hear whiffs of scandals in high office, but there was never any hint of anything like that at Busbys'.

I worked at Busbys' from 1947 to 1959 in the staff office where everything pertaining to the staff was dealt with. We arranged all the holiday rotas, we had staff up to the office to give them their rises, and we marked about four registers, which took over two hours every morning. Then at the end of the morning I would take a list into Mr. Gerald so we could see at a glance the new absentees so we could see if any department was understaffed, particularly the sales floor – because the whole object was that you never kept customers waiting; the customer comes first. And we had a lot of very nice ladies who didn't want full time work, but would come and work during holidays, Christmas, and sales times. If we could get a message to them they would come in and work from eleven a.m. to three p.m. to cover over the lunchtime, so that departments were never too short of staff.

One day Mr. Gerald said he would like an analysis of all the days lost during the year. This was a huge job to collate, so he said we'll have these categories: rheumatism, arthritis and lumbago; influenza, pneumonia and bronchitis; ulcers, piles and haemorrhoids; liver, kidney and bladder; and he said that should cover it! We hadn't heard of gynaecology in those days!

I used to go sick visiting because this was all part of staff welfare. I could ring down and get a car and visit people. I would talk to them. We had, for example, one lady who worked in the kitchen and she had been in hospital. The people who worked in the kitchen were paid Wages Council rates, but they were often very poor. I went to the address and found that she lived on an attic landing. She didn't even have a proper bed. Once we knew about her situation we could help her: Busbys' found her a bedsit somewhere else. But in those days people were very proud and didn't ask for help.

Busbys' tried to appeal to a wide range of Bradfordians. Brown Muffs in Bradford was, let's say, a 'posher' type of shop, but a lot of people didn't feel comfortable going in there. People dressed up to go to Brown Muffs; if I went in, for example, I wouldn't go in there without wearing a hat! People dressed up to a certain extent to go

Busbys' dinner dance (L-R) Jean Marshall (née Denby), Mr Howe,
Miss Virr, Miss McCamont, Mr and Mrs Radford

into Busbys' too, but they felt more comfortable there; the staff made them comfortable. The staff were trained how to deport themselves and how to speak to customers; for example, if you worked with the public we didn't like you biting your nails, and you never shouted across to another assistant. They got a very good training in customer relations, and if they had worked at Busbys' they could walk into a job anywhere else.

Miss Mitchell, the Personnel Director, was a big influence on staff training. She was an unmarried lady, very straight, and very straight-forward. She and the Directors led good lives; they were good people. When I look back on them, they all seemed to be people of integrity: very honest; not 'flash', they were sincere.

The impression I had of Mr. Ernest was that he was a gentleman. He was always immaculate; very straight, very courteous, polite and well-mannered. The three sons complemented each other very well. Mr. Arthur liked to be about the store talking to everyone and helping the buyers. Mr. Eric oversaw much of the artistic and advertising work; he was a small, dapper man, a fun person and a very nice man. They were all very visible to staff too; they had their own desks in the admin area. Mr. Gerald was the Managing Director and the bulk of responsibility fell on his shoulders. He was the one who drove the business: a very clever man; very good with figures. He didn't suffer fools gladly – and he expected the best from everybody. But he was very fair and had quite a sense of humour.

All the Directors liked a little bit of drama. When they had the Grotto, for example, they would dress up as Santa Claus; and when Santa came it stopped Bradford as there were thousands lining the route. The family loved to be out in amongst the crowd feeling the excitement and hearing the comments.

People in Bradford have good memories of Busbys'; the customer mattered in those days. The buyers went buying with Bradford customers in mind, and when the stock came in the assistant would contact a customer who they thought would like it.

In retrospect Busbys' meant a tremendous amount to me. It was my job, it was my work, and I loved it.
Jean Marshall (née Denby)

Staff canteen on top floor at Busbys'

Staff Canteen

There were lots of other juniors and many of us used to take lunch and tea breaks together in the canteen on the top floor. In those days we had lift attendants and we found them very amusing to look at, especially one very tall military looking gentleman who had a painted-on moustache. Yes, we would all stand alongside him to check this out and then fall into fits of giggles when we got out of the lift. The food was to us at that time (1965) wonderful, such delicacies as steak and kidney pudding, treacle sponge, and all those stodgy foods that us teenagers loved then. **Maureen Wallis** (formerly Kenny)

Fountain Hall

When Fountain Hall was built we used to have work dances there. We bought long dresses and thought ourselves the goods! We had some good times, and went to each other's weddings; it was a good, happy place!

Jean O'Hara

Fountain Hall

the Store with the friendly welcome

Programme for Fountain Hall. The venue where Busbys' held social events

_ys_

PRIVATE PARTIES

HALL

, BRADFORD

Available

. . . . . . SEATING CAPACITY 350
. . . . . . SEATING CAPACITY 250

OM OR FOR SMALLER FUNCTIONS

. . . . . . SEATING CAPACITY 150

DANCE FLOOR, MODERN KITCHENS
PMENT HAS ALSO BEEN INSTALLED

20364 & 20306

ED RENDEZVOUS FOR

ONS   WHIST DRIVES
S   BRIDGE DRIVES

REN'S PARTIES

LASS CATERING IS ESSENTIAL

STRAY, WHO WILL BE DELIGHTED TO SHOW VISITORS ROUND THE PREMISES
23456.

L A N E   ⋆   B R A D F O R D

Fountain Hall brochure

Hairdressing salon

Hairdressing Salon

In 1941 I commenced employment at Busbys' – 15/- a week, with 5/- war bonus. I was in the Hairdressing Department and loved every minute of it. What a treat when Santa arrived – the buzz would go round – he was on his way. We would leave our clients and dash onto the roof to watch the event – and coming down with dirty hands and overalls. Sometimes at lunchtime a crowd of us would grab a sandwich, get a trolley bus to the park and row to the middle of the lake to eat. **Phyllis Seage**

I worked at Busbys' from 1946 to 1956. I went there as a hairdressing apprentice, and my starting wage was 17/6d a week. In those days you didn't go to college; Busbys' trained you, and we used to have a late night on a Thursday and you could bring your friends and family in to practise your hairdressing on. I trained for 5 years.

I settled in very well. Busbys' was always very friendly, and I found it a very clean place; you never saw bits on the floor! The Busby family themselves always spoke to you and acknowledged us, were always friendly to us, and that rubbed off on us; made us the same way, and made us courteous and friendly to our customers. We weren't given any specific training in customer relations; it was something you just picked up by example: if the boss can do it, I can do it.

I was very happy in the hairdressing department; I can't remember ever having an argument or being upset, and we made many friends among the staff.

The hairdressing salon was on the top floor. There was a beauty counter and a lounge for customers. There was also a manicure bar to do client's nails. There was also a chiropodist – Harry Midgley – in my time, and next to him, a beautician's room. Then there were hairdressing cubicles, left and right and eventually an open salon was opened, which was all the rage then. There were around 30 trained hairdressers, plus juniors.

Every apprentice worked with a senior hairdresser. I worked with a Miss Gill who was lovely; she smoked her head off, but was a brilliant Marcel-waver, which you don't hear of these days; she was good to work with.

We had a receptionist called Miss Heap and she took all the apprentices under her wing and made sure we did all our cleaning and kept us on our toes!

There's a saying that 'you get what you pay for' and with Busbys' you found good, nice things to buy. **Jean O'Hara**

Fur department

Fur Department

I worked in the Fur Department as a junior. I started there in 1971. Mr. Speight was my manager; he was a fantastic man. I looked up to him. I was only 15 years old. I spent hours cleaning the display cabinets that they kept the expensive furs in. I had an Assistant Manager too. Her name was Margaret; she was only about 20 at the time we worked together, but she seemed so much older to me then. We had lots of laughs.

One day Margaret didn't come to work so there was just me and Mr. Speight. At lunchtime he had to leave me on my own. He said if anyone came to try on a fur I had to get the manager from the fur alterations department. Guess what! An elderly couple came to try a coat on as the husband was treating her for her 50th anniversary; money no object! Well I thought 'I can do this on my own'. I did. I sold a squirrel fur coat for £359. This was a great deal of money in 1972. The lady also tried a mink coat – £1000 – my heart was beating. But the mink didn't suit her at all; she chose the squirrel. I then called the manager to come down to do the personal alterations to her coat. They used to make it fit like a glove and embroider their name inside and put their address in the coat somewhere secret.

There was also the fur storage. It was like a massive cold storage room kept at a low temperature. Ladies brought their coats in for the summer so they wouldn't get moth eaten. What memories! **Jackie Cox**

The fur room was a very happy place to work; they were all lovely people, and I absolutely loved working with the furs, including minks. For me, as a junior, it was way beyond my means to own a fur coat, so I was getting to handle one of these beautiful garments. People brought their coats out of cold storage and would want them modernised, so it was amazing to see how the coats could be made into a totally different garment through the expertise of the people in the fur workroom. People came from miles around, as Busbys' was renowned for the Fur Department and for the fur workroom, and they knew they would get a first class alteration job done there.
Ruth Ackroyd

Lamsom Room/Accounts department

The Lamson System

I worked in the Lamson room for a while. When you bought something at Busbys' the assistant would put the money in a little numbered tube in a pipe and it was zapped through to a central point – the Lamson Room – where two cashiers put the change back into the tube; my role was to pick up the tubes and zap them back to the right department. The department tubes would all be numbered, so, for example, number 6 would be Haberdashery. I worked there at Christmas time when it was so busy; the tubes were coming down there fast and furious, so sometimes there would be four of us just collecting and sending these tubes back and forth. The tubes would be sucked up the pipes with a tremendous whoosh! I would say from the tube arriving and sending it back took just two minutes, and in the meantime the goods would be being packed beautifully on the department, so it didn't seem that long to the customer. **Ruth Ackroyd**

Ten miles of tubing was used to take the money from each department to the Accounts Room from where the change was returned.

82

BUSBYS'

AMATEUR DRAMATIC SOCIETY

PRESENTS

WHEN WE ARE MARRIED

By J. B. PRIESTLEY

AT

FOUNTAIN HALL, BRADFORD

ON

TUESDAY and WEDNESDAY

October 30th and 31st, 1956

Commencing at 7-15 p.m.

RESERVED SEATS 3/-   **UNRESERVED 1/6**

Proceeds to the Drapers' Institution and Cottage Homes

Staff Romances

My husband started in August 1945 in the Display Department. We did all our courting behind number 6 lift. **Laura Pollard**

I worked in the Advertising Department in the 1960s as assistant to the Manager. In 1965 I was invited to join the Cottage Homes Ball Committee by Gerald C. Busby (GCB) who was Chairman of the Committee. Eventually I attended the Ball at Fountain Hall and was asked to dance by a good looking man who turned out to be on the Maintenance Staff and who eventually became my husband. So I can truthfully say that GCB played Cupid on that occasion. **Jean Redshaw** (née Glen)

Busbys' was very strict if anybody was doing a 'bit of bothering' – going after someone's husband, or vice versa – all of a sudden they wouldn't be there. So you would say 'where's so-and-so this morning', and they'd say 'Oh, she's left'. It would turn out that she had been 'bothering' with someone else's husband in another department, and they wouldn't tolerate that, so she had to go. But a lot of firms in Bradford were like that at that time. **Jean O'Hara.**

Office Memories

I have very fond memories of the whole Busbys' experience: from joining the typing pool at 18, then quickly into the Staff Department, then into Admin under the 'eagle eye' of Mr. Gerald, who over time came to be a paternal friend. After Mr. Gerald retired I used to go to Crow Trees, his home, and do secretarial work for him. He was no longer the 'ogre', but a very agreeable boss and friend. Having a mid-morning sherry whilst taking dictation – lovely! **Margaret Sheard** (née Day/Shepherd)

I worked in the large open plan office 1948–54 on the Burroughs accounting machine. The comptometer girls worked alongside and there was a dictaphone with a connection to the accounts desk where customers came to pay their statements. **K. Swaine** (née Connell)

Busbys' was very imposing: big, in a very nice building, and the departments were spotless. People could get off the bus at Busbys' and spend half the day there; you could buy anything.

I worked at Busbys' from 1950 to 1956 as a shorthand/typist in the Credit Manager's office. It was a wonderful place; I was so happy to go there and every day was a pleasure. I had some wonderful times: I was in the Dramatic Society, the Concert Party. And there was a cricket team, dominoes team; all sorts. The management were very supportive with all the groups that we had there.

The friendliness of Busbys' made it special, and we all knew one another there in all the departments. In fact, I met my husband there. He was a gent's hairdresser in the basement, and he was in the Concert Party too; that's how we met. But he got lung problems so he came out of hairdressing, and was made a Floor Manager. He loved his job as well.

I remember Mr. Ernest. He used to come with a bow tie; always immaculate. He used to walk through different departments; everybody knew him, acknowledged him, and he would always have a word. So the friendly atmosphere came from the Busby family. The managers expected all the staff to do their best – and everybody did. **Doreen Wilson**

Perfumery department, 1938

Fabric department, 1954

China department, 1938

Miscellaneous Staff Memories

I worked in the China Department before the war and I was also a Button Boy. After the war I could not go back to work at Busbys', as I was badly wounded at Monte Casino. I am now 91 years old and I have happy memories of my time at the store. **George Hudson**

My husband and myself both worked at Busbys' from 1952 until 1959 when we left to go to Canada. I think we were the only married couple employed by Busbys'. This was caused by a slip-up in the employment office. As we had both been hired they kindly kept their promise. When we went to Expo in Brussels in 1959 we mentioned to Mr. Gerald that we thought the Manager of the Window Display Department might get some ideas if he went to the Expo. This he did, and Mr. Gerald gave us a very nice camera as a reward for the suggestion. **Annie Paulton**

I worked at Busbys' 1953–4 in the Ladies Coat and Suit Department and loved the atmosphere on the showroom floor. We were all addressed as 'Mrs.', 'Miss', etc. and we always addressed the customers as 'Madam'. **Anonymous**

I worked at Busbys' from 1966–69 on the Knitting Wool and Haberdashery counter. Everyone made me feel so welcome. Just coming out of school at 15 and going to work was quite an experience, but they turned out to be the best three years of my life. I will always remember them with fondness and the many friends I made. **Marion Charles**

Lingerie department, 1938

I worked at Busbys' from 1955 to 1959; I was fifteen when I started. This was my first job and I started in the Lingerie Department. There was a really good atmosphere there – because you were well-treated. The Busby family came round daily and spoke to you and got to know you – you mattered. They sold all sorts of lingerie, and it was a very interesting department. They did train you, but it wasn't formal training; you were trained in the department with the buyer and alongside the experienced sales staff; the buyer at the time was just like a mother to me.

You had to get to know everything you sold so that you knew what you were talking about. I wasn't allowed to serve for quite a while, and the sales went in order of seniority from the first, second, third sales assistants. But if they were talking to a customer, you might then have a chance to sell something. But if I sold something and they didn't, they could get quite annoyed! I learned a lot from working at Busbys' – about customer relations and selling – and I learned how to get on with other people; it was a very happy time.

I joined the Concert Party group in 1956 with two other girls and we had a tap-dancing routine going. We used to do a show at the staff concert, and on a Wednesday half day closing we would go to the Veteran's Hut in Manningham Park, or OAP groups, and to other places all over Bradford to give concerts. I also took the main part in 'Sailor Beware', which was very exciting. This was the start of my lifetime interest in the theatre. You get confidence from doing things like this in front of people. **Dorothy West**

Window display – Special Fabric Event

I worked at Busbys' from 1959 to 1963 and my main job was working in the dressmaking and alterations department from 8.30a.m. to 5.30p.m. as an apprentice under Miss Sutcliffe and Miss Hurley; I started on £2/10/- a week. I'd always wanted to sew, as I took after my grandmother. In those days starting as an apprentice in alterations meant learning all the basics and doing all the general 'muggings' jobs. You learned the old-fashioned – the proper way – from scratch, like doing button-holes by hand; and I'm glad I did. It was a skill you never forgot; it stays with you for life. I had my own shop eventually, and even now I do hand-finishing, rather than use a machine.

Busbys' to me, as a youngster, was such a magnificent building; it looked so spectacular; it felt a grand place to work, just like going to Buckingham Palace! It was just like when you are buying a house and you get a feeling that you are going to be happy there; well, Busbys' just felt right for me. I was very happy there.

The three Busby sons would wander round the store and would always stop and talk. They would ask me how I was getting on with my apprenticeship. They were very kind and really cared about every single member of staff; they knew everyone's name. If any member of staff had difficulties, through illness or financially, they would try and help you. They took notice of your personal needs; you weren't just an employee, they went the extra mile for you. One hot summer day, when we were absolutely melting in the workroom, Miss Hurley came in and told us that Mr. Gerald had said we could all have an ice cream on him! It was just little things like that that are special, and that you remember for a long time. **Ruth Ackroyd**

Childrenswear department

In the mid sixties, as a student, I had a vacation job at Busbys' to pay for piano lessons. We clocked in and out, and ate our lunches in the staff canteen upstairs. I earned £8 a week working in the Ladies' Exclusive Knitwear Department on the first floor – not the slightly less prestigious ground-floor Knitwear Stall. The stock was kept in drawers inside the counter, and clean, well-manicured hands were obligatory as we showed customers a selection of garments, spreading them out on the counter. To this day I still fold shirts and tops symmetrically, the way I was taught at Busbys', so they would fit neatly back in the drawers and look good the next time they were spread out.

Account customers were especially well treated. For those paying cash, we sent the money to the cash office in small cylinders that were inserted into the Lamson Paragon network, where they were whisked off by suction to the cash office. A few minutes later the customer's change and receipt came back, and those few moments' wait were the occasion for polite conversation with customers, many of whom bought regularly. Too late, I managed to grasp the etiquette involved in the hierarchical system, in which 'first sales' approached customers, and other colleagues, in order, were then directed to various serving and other duties. Everything was polite, quiet and businesslike: not at all like the frantic noisy mania of much of today's fashion retailing. **Judy Blezzard**

Record department

I worked at Busbys' from 1965–9 and remember the friendly, family environment. The staff looked after each other. **Sylvia Parratt** (née Greenwood)

Saturday jobs at Busbys' were prized. After several months serving screws, lampshades and curtain rails at Woolworths in Darley Street, 10/- for the day, I moved up to Busbys' to sell shoes for 15/- a day. We all wore… "a nice grey dress, dear, and black shoes please. Don't lean on the counter, look expectant (she didn't mean it…?) as if you really WANT customers!" **Kath Healey** (née Bradley)

I came to work at Busbys' between 1959–62. I was 15 years old. It was a wonderful time in my life. I first worked down in the basement as a Junior in the Inexpensive Fashions Department. I spent hours ironing all the dresses for the sales (today I still hate ironing!) then I transferred to the first floor to work with a lovely lady – she was Billie Whitelaw's mother. I then went to work in the Record Department in Drewton Street and I met my first love, Irvin Smith, who worked in the ticket office. **Linda Wilkinson**

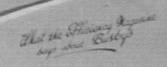

That the Printing Presses
say about Busbys

"FEW OTHER STORES IN ENGLAND
IF ANY ARE GROWING FASTER
THAN BUSBYS.

FIVE YEARS AGO THIS STORE HAD
37,600 SQUARE FEET
OF FLOOR SPACE.

IT WAS ENLARGED

NOW THIS STORE IS ENLARGING AGAIN
AND TO HAVE
125,237 SQUARE FEET
OF FLOOR SPACE."

1908 XXV

W
BIRT

3

£1

MODEL of
BUSBYS
IN
1908

A Story Without Words

...ars of Progress 195...

SCALE MODEL of BUSBYS

1935

Busbys Cafe
SERVED
619319
CUSTOMERS
Last Year

Window display – celebrating 27 years, 1935

THE RENSHAW
CHALLENGE CUP

MODEL
of
Busbys 28th
BIRTHDAY CAKE
Made on the Premises

FREE PORTIONS
OF THE ACTUAL CAKE
Served to all our
Café Customers
Last Saturday

Book department, 1938

Although I worked at Busbys' for only three and a half years (1955–58) there was a lovely atmosphere throughout the store. I recall the friendliness of the Directors with Mr. Arthur and Mr. Eric walking through the Gown Department regularly. Mr. Paul often remained in the department for a friendly chat. Mr. Ernest was constantly charming and talkative and I still cherish a cosmetic tray he gave me on the occasion of my wedding in 1957. **Mrs. Pepperday**

I worked in the Toy Department 1955–1956. Having married a Bradford man in Dublin, and come to live in Bradford, this was the first job I took. Having been there a couple of weeks, Mr. Gerald Busby approached me one morning and asked if I was the young lady from Ireland and asked me to go with him to another department to be introduced to another Irish girl who had also joined the staff. In such a large establishment I was amazed to think how much thought was given to an individual. **Anonymous**

Window display, 1936

McCall
Fashion Parade

AIDS TO HOME DRESSMAKERS

1. ENORMOUS SELECTION OF PATTERNS
2. CUTTING OUT SERVICE
3. CUTTING OUT & TACKING UP
4. BUTTON & BELT MAKING
5. PLEATING
6. INEXPENSIVE DRESSMAKING
7. SKIRT MAKING

Window display, 1951

Window display – Eugene Curl

Display Department

I was privileged to be given a position in the Ticket-writing Office attached to the Display Department. As part of the display team I can boast of having been one of 'Santa's little helpers'. When the theme, design and planning of the Wonderland had taken place, one of my tasks as a junior usually resulted being up to my elbows in buckets of glue size and whitening, cutting and pasting large sheets of grey-coloured paper over a wire-mesh base to form the 'mountains' and fairyland rocks. Later, when they were dry, they were painted in delicate colours and enhanced by cleverly placed lighting, providing Santa with his magical kingdom.

I recall John Busby designing and creating a wire-framed aeroplane, which circled over part of the Kingdom to the amazement of wide-eyed children. The Ticket Office, part of the Display Department where I was assistant to Mr. Hanson (in those days you never addressed your head of department by a Christian name) was the room where departmental heads in the main store sent their staff, usually a junior, to order price tickets for any new or replacement items on their displays. These had to be supplied quickly. As ticket writers we produced all requirements by paint and brush and in the colour and background card dictated by the department's floor location. **Keith Sivyer**

I worked in the Display Department from 1965–71 and enjoyed my time at this super store. Great times getting the Grotto ready for the Christmas season, starting in September with Father Christmas practising his trumpet ready for the parade to the store. A great start to my working life. **Gillian Bannister** (née Griffin)

Queuing outside Busbys' for first day of sales

Morecambe visitors returning home by bus, c1931

July sales, 1948

When I left school I was taken on as a junior sales assistant. The department I worked in was Ladies Knitwear. When the January Sales were on we arrived to find huge queues of people right along the front of the building. The manager, a Mr. Smith, I think, stood on a chair before the doors opened at 9.00a.m. to give us all a pep talk. Then they opened the doors and in rushed hordes of ladies. It was quite scary, a bit like a herd of buffaloes.
Maureen Wallis

Busbys' Sales

Busbys' sales became a byword. I was so keyed up I used to hire a taxi to take me to work on the first day in case my car failed. We achieved a popular routine: at 7.30a.m. a free cup of tea was given to the first 75 in the queue, then the first 50 customers were asked to write down the particular bargain they were after (each window was numbered and the goods clearly marked). At 9a.m. G. [Gerald] blew his whistle and called, "let battle commence!"

Only one customer at a time was allowed through the doors for the first twenty minutes. These individuals, often having queued for hours, were met by a sales assistant who, in conjunction with display staff, produced the required goods. The sales staff was augmented by office and workroom personnel – anyone who had their name down early enough, as it was a much sought-after experience for people who usually worked behind the scenes. The atmosphere was light-hearted, no one was injured in a stampede, and we were always elated at the end of the day.

Eric Busby: (from 'Letters from Eric Busby to his Grandchildren')

Busbys' front façade collapsing onto Manningham Lane

The End of Busbys'

Busbys' is engulfed in flames

Busbys' and Debenhams merged in 1958 and successfully continued trading under the Busbys' name for the next fifteen years. In March 1973 Debenhams announced that all its stores would be re-branded with their name. All references to Busbys' and its trademarks disappeared, which caused dismay and protest in the city. Trade continued, but in 1978 Debenhams announced it was closing the Bradford store. Later that year a proposal was made to demolish the Victorian facade and replace it with a modern building. This again was met with a public outcry and it was agreed that the grand old exterior would stay. However, on the 30th August 1979 a fire broke out, which rapidly spread, and gutted the entire building.

****

The last seconds of the famous Busbys' clock

Firemen fighting the blaze

I remember the absolute shock of seeing Busbys' go up in flames. I was walking into town and saw the massive conflagration as I approached. I knew that Busbys' (then Debenhams) had closed by then, but I can clearly recall the feeling of sadness as the flames engulfed the lovely old Victorian building. **Mae Price**

While working at Rackham's department store I left work to hear sirens. I went up Manningham Lane and saw the spectacular end to the Busbys' building: walls collapsing and fireman at risk of losing their lives. It really was a sad end to a great Bradford landmark. **A.N. Partridge**

We saw the smoke from Manningham Lane and heard about the fire on the news. It was terrible; that beautiful, beautiful building gone. It was the end of an era. **Doreen Wilson**

It was a sad end; very emotional in the city, but I think the family and Bradford people were glad in a way to see the store go out in a big dramatic blaze rather then fall into dereliction. **Jean Marshall**

Firemen outside a smouldering Busbys'

I could hardly expect to have had warning about the next event in the history of the building, nevertheless on 30th August 1979 someone *did* phone me. "Busbys' is on fire!" they said.

My first reaction was that it would not be a serious episode because of the sprinkler system, so it was in a light-hearted mood that I drove from my home in Ilkley via the moor road to Bradford. It was a beautiful evening at the end of a day of heat-wave. When I saw a whiff of smoke from Hawksworth I even found myself hoping they would keep the fire going until I got there.

But what horror! I arrived just after a third of the front façade had fallen into Manningham Lane. Flames were belching from all windows that still remained perpendicular. The roof and tower had gone. My old office had crashed down through these three burnt-out floors to the red hot basement. There was a terrifying firestorm in the air all round in which nearly one hundred firemen from all over West Yorkshire were working, together with masses of police for traffic and crowd control. Manningham Lane was closed and a crowd of many thousands was cordoned off to a safe distance. I got through the barriers by approaching from Eldon Place into Hallfield Road – in time to see the Pater's office burst into flame.

Burnt out Busbys' and remains of the clock

Three human kindly incidents remain in my memory of that evening: a pretty policewoman telling me to get behind the barrier 'Sir'. I showed her my card and told her about my father's office. She said how sorry she was, how awful for me, and let me stay. Then, I remember one of the old kitchen staff spotting me and shouting elatedly "At least that's the end of Debenhams too, Mr. Eric!" I asked another person I half-recognised, who was in tears, "Were you one of us?" She said she was once "*Your* fairy in *your* Grotto".

Of course I went to G.'s [Gerald] home to share the agony and phone my family. And when I could, I went to the City Fire Department to ask how the sprinkler system could have failed. The short answer was that the water had been cut off. It transpired that the fire had started simultaneously in all the widely spaced staircases. A classic arson give-away, though nothing could be proved. It was a poor show and a wicked waste in their opinion.

So the famous Victorian building was burnt to a mass of twisted metal and rubble in less than three hours. I cannot dwell on this sad ending except to say that it was less distressing than the empty building had been. And mind you, I did think that as a fire it was the best ever! A dramatic, super-magnificent finale.

Eric Busby: (from 'Letters from Eric Busby to his Grandchildren')

Bugsby's

The Store with the Friendly Welcome

An Exhibition at
Bradford Industrial Musuem

1st December 2007 - 24 February 2008

FREE ADMISSION

Bradford Industrial Museum Exhibition Programme

108

The Busbys' Exhibition

Busbys' — The Store with the Friendly Welcome — by night.

Exhibition postcard, 2007

In late 2007 and into 2008 Bradford Industrial Museum mounted an exhibition on the history of Busbys'. This was one of the most successful events staged there, attracting over 17,000 visitors. Over 300 visitors wrote their personal memories of Busbys' on the Memories Board or in the Memories Book provided.

Pat Laycock, daughter of Eric Busby, later wrote her account of the background, staging, and impact of this event.

****

During the Christmas period of 2006/ 2007 Amy and I visited a very small display of photographs of Father (Busby) Christmas at Bradford Industrial Museum. It was apparent, from a review Amy had read in the *Telegraph & Argus*, that this was creating a great deal of interest, so she had contacted Mike Callaghan, curator at the Museum, and asked if we could meet. Mike was interested to hear our reminiscences, experiences and especially to realise how many artefacts and information we could supply about the history of the Busbys' Store; he was beginning to think a large exhibition might be a possibility.

It is perhaps relevant that in 2006 (after a great deal of sorting out) Amy, Paul and I had deposited a large box of photographs, with explanatory text, with the Bradford Archives Department (Bradford Library), documenting the history of Busbys' from its inception in 1908. This was following a feeling we had that they should be placed in safe-keeping for posterity. We consulted all the other cousins and Peter Busby and they agreed we should go ahead. It seemed unfair to burden the young generation with deciding what should be done with them; not only that, but they could not be expected to know who or what the photographs represented.

Santa Busby Claus and Mother Christmas leaving Lister Park, c1950s

Coincidentally Bradford Museums had recently purchased a vast archive of photographs from the family of the industrial photographer CH Wood. This collection included very many photographs of Busbys', especially of the Grotto, but including photographs of the departments, the café and various personalities who worked in the store in the days before it was sold to Debenhams.

Amy and I brought Paul along to the subsequent meetings at the Museum and his knowledge, plus merchandising experience, became an important input to the possibility of an exhibition. Mike, and his team, were by now very enthusiastic about the whole concept and their energy, experience and inspiration became a constant source of amazement to us three Busbys!

Mike and the team came up with the idea of having a major exhibition in the winter of 2007/8, running from 1st December to 24th February. The store had been founded 100 years before this, and Ernest Busby, the Pater, died on 1st December 50 years previously. These events were quite coincidental to the exhibition but held extraordinary significance for the family.

The exhibition eventually kicked off with a Grand Opening on Saturday 1st December with the Lord Mayor in attendance. Very many members of the family, former members of staff and friends turned up for this event; Paul made a splendid opening speech, and the atmosphere was electric: so many people wanting to re-introduce themselves and so many memories to share! The Museum had gone to great lengths to give the show a Christmas theme as Father (Busby) Christmas was probably the most abiding memory for most the people. A festive tree decorated with Busby Logo cards tied on by red ribbon, Father Christmas throwing out sweets to the crowd, suspended red baubles from the ceiling, and, in the Museum café menus which were printed on the familiar beige card which Busbys' used, with the logo on top – just like the originals in the famous café. Busby artefacts took pride of place – from carved newel-post Busby-soldier-heads, to crockery, boxes, stained-glass panels, toy vans and many other items. The family had brought most of these artefacts in and had managed to unearth objects ranging from fur coats and silver foundation-laying trowels to lead soldiers – even humble paper bags. A great many family or Store historical documents which were of relevance were also on display, dating

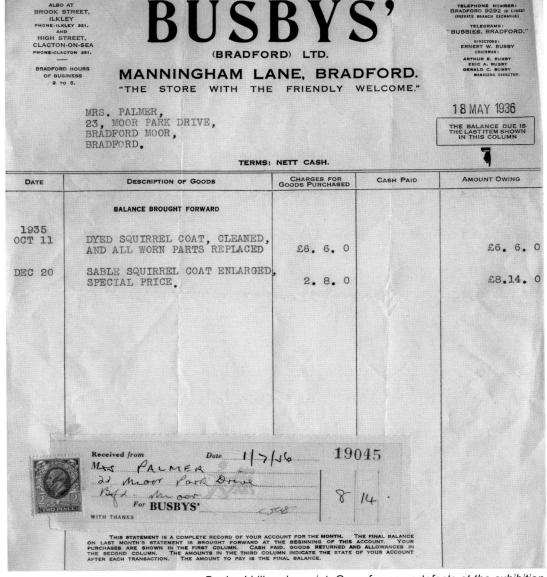

BUSBYS'

(BRADFORD) LTD.

ALSO AT
BROOK STREET,
ILKLEY
PHONE-ILKLEY 331.
AND
HIGH STREET,
CLACTON-ON-SEA
PHONE-CLACTON 291.

BRADFORD HOURS
OF BUSINESS
9 TO 6.

MANNINGHAM LANE, BRADFORD.
"THE STORE WITH THE FRIENDLY WELCOME."

TELEPHONE NUMBER:
BRADFORD 9292 (6 LINES)
(PRIVATE BRANCH EXCHANGE)

TELEGRAMS:
"BUSBIES. BRADFORD."

DIRECTORS:
ERNEST W. BUSBY
CHAIRMAN:
ARTHUR E. BUSBY
ERIC A. BUSBY
GERALD C. BUSBY
MANAGING DIRECTOR.

MRS. PALMER,
23, MOOR PARK DRIVE,
BRADFORD MOOR,
BRADFORD.

18 MAY 1936

THE BALANCE DUE IS
THE LAST ITEM SHOWN
IN THIS COLUMN

TERMS: NETT CASH.

DATE	DESCRIPTION OF GOODS	CHARGES FOR GOODS PURCHASED	CASH PAID	AMOUNT OWING
	BALANCE BROUGHT FORWARD			
1935 OCT 11	DYED SQUIRREL COAT, CLEANED, AND ALL WORN PARTS REPLACED	£6. 6. 0		£6. 6. 0
DEC 20	SABLE SQUIRREL COAT ENLARGED, SPECIAL PRICE.	2. 8. 0		£8.14. 0

Received from _____ Date 1/7/36 _____ 19045

M̶r̶s̶ PALMER
23 Moor Park Drive
Bfd. Moor _____
For BUSBYS' _____ 8 /14 .
WITH THANKS

TWO PENCE

THIS STATEMENT IS A COMPLETE RECORD OF YOUR ACCOUNT FOR THE MONTH. THE FINAL BALANCE ON LAST MONTH'S STATEMENT IS BROUGHT FORWARD AT THE BEGINNING OF THIS ACCOUNT. YOUR PURCHASES ARE SHOWN IN THE FIRST COLUMN. CASH PAID. GOODS RETURNED AND ALLOWANCES IN THE SECOND COLUMN. THE AMOUNTS IN THE THIRD COLUMN INDICATE THE STATE OF YOUR ACCOUNT AFTER EACH TRANSACTION. THE AMOUNT TO PAY IS THE FINAL BALANCE.

Busbys' bill and receipt. One of many artefacts at the exhibition

back to Ernest's apprentice days in London. (Incidentally these documents had not been deposited with the Bradford Archive Service as they were self-explanatory and would hold significance for future generations).

The museum staff had made very large window blind/screens of Busby photographs from the CH Wood archive. These eye-catching, naturally lit, images set the historical scene perfectly, and were complemented by other enlarged photographs round the walls, and videos running throughout the show. In addition to a big visitors' book there were tables with paper and writing materials for reminiscences. This idea proved very popular – leading to memory boards with hundreds of papers pinned on them. The Museum is hoping to put these into book form, which should prove entertaining indeed, especially the ones from the less scrupulous people who were not averse to stealing a thing or two then, or confessing that they did so now!

As well as the predominantly Busby angle, thanks to the collection of the Museum Service, the exhibition contained clothes and artefacts which would have been on sale at the time of the Store's operation, giving interesting examples of what was in the shops as well as prices.

The Museum staff had also arranged for media coverage which was enthusiastically taken up by the press and TV; there was even a *Museum of the Week* recommendation in *The Times*! Amy, Paul and I had a lot of fun co-operating with the journalists, giving interviews and reminiscing. They seemed to be fascinated to learn that members of the Busby family were still around (alive?)!

B U S B Y S
THE STORE WITH THE FRIENDLY WELCOME
A special dedication

Many years ago, though it doesn't seem that long,
We were part of a happy, bustling throng,
In a store of smiling faces, with a welcome there for all –
A bright and shining atmosphere that never failed to call.

And people came from many walks of life along the Lane –
For its name was known by one and all, through sunshine, snow and rain.
And we recall the "Governor", – resplendent, smart and trim
Walking through this wonderland, which was all because of him.

And his sons – all three of them – each dedicated too,
Carried on the long tradition, welcoming me and you,
And a special treat we now recall, which happened once a year –
For Santa in his Grotto would magically appear,

And seeing children's faces – every girl and every boy –
Was really unforgettable, a special Christmas joy.
And then we had our Concerts, with laughter, songs and fun,
And a Drama Group presented plays – a winner every one!

And everyone was happy, that's the thought that I hold dear,
For despite the changes through the years the message is so clear
That friendliness and caring are important all life through,
And on reflection at this time, we know that it's so true.

For now old friends can meet again, but in a different place,
Recalling friendships old and new, with each familiar face.
For memories of happy days are brought to life today –
This Special Anniversary of our " gathering in May".

And though that familiar building still stands erect and tall,
It's empty now and quiet, but for all that – to us all
It holds a very special part of life all those years ago,
With a special kind of family, we're all so proud to know.

Doreen Wilson,
April 1979.

A special dedication

ALL FABRICS IN THIS WINDOW ARE MANUFACTURED IN OUR OWN CITY

Window display, Kirkgate store

On 27th January another amazing Grand Event took place: "Memories are Made of This". Over two thousand people turned up, including just about all the extended Busby family. Jean Marshall, née Denby, who worked in the Staff Office, from approximately 1950–60, gave two talks about working in the store, which were both packed out, with standing room at the back! Jean, who has perfected this talk of hers over several years in order to give it to local organisations, is able to put a perspective on the business which would be an impossible task for a member of the family. Her angle is very flattering as well as being historically interesting. It was quite an emotional experience for the family.

It was interesting to the older Busbys to see the astonished reaction of the young members of the family. They had, of course, heard about the store and the pivotal role it played in family life but really had no idea of its influence on Bradford's shopping habits, its size or of the employment it gave to so many people. It needed this exhibition to make it come alive for them.

So, finally, the show closed at the end of the afternoon of 24th February 2008. Over 17,500 people had visited compared to 9,710 for the same period in the previous year. I treasure many memories of friends, as well as people I hardly know, making a point of writing, phoning and telling me how much they had enjoyed it, and, incidentally the whole of the ethos of the Industrial Museum. I came to realise that people were remembering Bradford as it used to be as well as 'The Store with the Friendly Welcome'. The end of the building and the business, i.e. the fire in August 1979, although shocking, would seem to have become anachronistic in more ways than one.

Pat Laycock, February 2008

Bradford Industrial Museum, 12th September 1977

Milestones of Busbys' Department Store

1908 — Founded by Ernest W. Busby

1910 — Staff 42

1914/18 — War

1918 — Ilkley shop opened

1919 — Kirkgate premises purchased

1924 — Part of Laycock's Café purchased and annexed

1926 — Leased and annexed property over next door premises

1928 — Leased and annexed property next door but one

1929 — Final year at Kirkgate store. Staff 150

1930 — Busbys' opened their doors on Manningham Lane

1930 — Remaining portion of Manningham Lane property purchased. Staff 250

1931 — Foundation stone Drewton Street extension laid by Amy Busby

1932 — Lord Mayor and Lady Mayoress opened third extension

1932 — Fabric Hall opened

1933 — Men's Shop opened

1934 — Lord Mayor and Lady Mayoress opened new main entrance and further extensions

1934 — Girls' Grammar School purchased

1934 — Springfield House portion of the Girls' Grammar School occupied

1934 — Purchase of property in Drewton Street

1935 — Amy Busby, Ernest's wife, died

1935 — Second extension in depth of Manningham Lane store

1935 — Opened new Fur Storage

1935 — Petrol Pump service opened

1935 — Staff 500

1937 — Power House and Laundry opened

1938 — Hallfield Road extension opened

1939 — Staff 800

1944 — Ernest Busby remarries, to Dorothy Paling.

1946	Purchased Hallfield House for use as Warehouse and Workrooms
1949	Dry Cleaning Department opened Ice Cream Factory opened Staff 900
1951	Fountain Street property purchased for Warehouses
1952	Hallfield House opened up for trading. Staff 1000
1953	Fourth floor added to main premises
1953	Buckleys' of Harrogate purchased from the John Lewis Partnership
1954	Fountain Hall opened as a Social Rendezvous, and extension to catering organisation
1954	Sites cleared and Car Parks constructed in Drewton Street
1956	New Petrol Station opened, enlargement to Car Park
1957	Hallfield Corner site purchased
1957	Hallfield Church (closed for worship 1956) purchased
1958	Fountain Hall extensions opened
1958	Manningham Lane display frontage extended on Hallfield Road corner
1958	Opening of building in Hallfield Road for Furniture Showrooms
1958	Another Car Park opened
1958	Friendly merger with Debenhams
1959	New Bedding Shop opened in Hallfield House
1959	Newly re-fitted Fashion Floor opened by Lord Mayor and Lady Mayoress
1960	Re-fitted Housewares Basement Department opened
1960	New Carpet Department completed
1960	New Soft Furnishings section, including the Net Shop, opened
1961	Ground floor finally completed after one year of work
1961	"The New Busbys'"
1973	Debenhams remove the Busbys' name and all stores nationwide are re-branded with the name Debenhams
1978	Debenhams close the store on Manningham Lane
1979	A spectacular fire completely destroys the store on Manningham Lane

Mr. G. C. Busby laying the Foundation

...e of Busbys' Power House, July 1937.

Postcard, 1937

Crowd outside Busbys', with Mr Baier on the right, celebrating the laying of the foundation stone for the Power House, 1937

Greengrocers department with carved Busby head on staircase, 1938

Busbys' store in Harrogate , 1954

Children's Hairdressing Salon, 1940

Busbys', Manningham Lane, Bradford, c1935

Bibliography

Bradford Industrial Museum. Personal memories from visitors to the 'Busbys' – The Store with the Friendly Welcome' exhibition held at Bradford Industrial Museum 1st December 2007 to 24th February 2008.

Busbys' (n/d). Busbys', *Bradford and Harrogate, a Brief History.* Bradford: Busbys'.

Busbys' (1958). *Busbys' The First Fifty Years, 1908–1958.* Bradford: Busbys'.

Busby, E.W. (1948). *A Personal Survey of the Past Forty Years.* Bradford: Busbys' (Bradford) Ltd.

Laycock, P. (Editor) (1995). *The Short One on the Right: Letters from Eric Busby to his Grandchildren.* Addingham (West Yorkshire): PL Publishing.

Private Collections: Amy Booth: archive material from her family collection; Paul Busby: archive material from his family collection; Pat Laycock: archive material from her family collection; Joan Marshall: archive material from her own collection.

CH Wood [Photographic Archive]. Owned by Bradford Museums Galleries and Heritage and currently stored at Bradford Industrial Museum.

Other material relating to the history of Busbys' can be found at the West Yorkshire Archives Service (Bradford), Bradford Central Library, Prince's Way, Bradford BD1 1NN. Telephone: 01274 435099.
Email: bradford@wyjs.org.uk

Endpaper: Aerial view of Busbys' on Manningham Lane, c1937